David

A Living in the Past

An East Anglian venture in antiques & bygones

An IMAGES publication

1

A Living in the Past

First published in Great Britain by Images Publications 1990

ISBN 0 948134 22 4

Images Publications Woolpit Suffolk IP30 9RP

Phototypeset in Baskerville by
Roda Typographics Ltd, Farringdon Road, London EC1M 3JB
Printed by
Whitstable Litho Printers Ltd, Millstrood, Whitstable, Kent CT5 3PP

A LIVING IN THE PAST

Contents

LOT 1: A Living in the Past.................. 7

LOT 2: A Girl called Jennifer..................17

LOT 3: Setting the Scene.....................25

LOT 4: Have a nice Day.....................38

LOT 5: A Funny Business....................53

LOT 6: A Gaggle of Geese....................65

LOT 7: Greenfingers.........................82

LOT 8: Sitting Pretty.........................90

LOT 9: A Broad Canvas......................99

LOT 10: Suffolk Beetles......................107

LOT 11: Full Cycle...........................115

LOT 12: On the Move........................121

LOT 13: Daily Rounds........................131

LOT 14: Low Tech. High Tech.................146

To Mary

FOREWORD

Although an adoptive East Anglian — having been born in Lincolnshire — I boldly claim regionality on the simple grounds of intimate and long acquaintance. My home is here, in the beautiful Waveney Valley, and I can imagine living nowhere else. It therefore gives me great pleasure to write the introduction to this book by David Hill, whose writing I have long enjoyed, and whose love of the region and its people is reflected so strongly in his work.

A joy of this book it strikes chords in the reader's mind. "Oh yes", we respond inwardly, "I know the place. That is exactly how it is". Reading it evokes thoughts of lazy hours spent browsing through antique shops in quiet market towns, and of gentle villages peacefully going about their business — still — while the thatcher and country carpenter work their skills, and poppies grow among the corn that ripples in a summer breeze.

"A Living in the Past" deals mainly with the years during which David and Mary Hill ran an antiques business, first in Suffolk and later, in association with their son, in Norfolk. For me, the book also prompts memories of being on the receiving end of more than one golden session of impromptu instruction — on anything from flower arranging to mole catching — from local experts long practised in their skills. For another joy of this book is the high regard in which all crafts, trades and artisans are held by the author, himself no mean craftsman in wood and furniture restoration.

He describes himself as "a rude carpenter", at his happiest when "crisp wood-shavings lay in drifts around the feet of the bench". David Hill's interest in all practical work, then, has led him to talk to many tradesmen about their skills over the years. The information thus relayed yields absorbing descriptions in this book of the traditional tools and working methods of occupations as diverse as pargeting and well-sinking.

But the book is about a lot more besides. We meet relatives, friends and customers, and we sometimes roam far afield. We hear old wives' tales and opinions, look in on family weddings, read fascinating snippets of local history and even learn how to identify an adder. Just like catalogues of the many house sales attended by the author over the years, the pages contain a striking diversity, a miscellany of the practical and the romantic.

Yet, unlike those items laid out bleakly for auction sale bereft of the warm, living quality once uniting them into the cohesive whole of a family home, the ''lots'' of David Hill's story are threaded together by a discernible strand of human happiness. What makes our lives happy? If asked, we might all readily list the obvious pillars — caring family, enough to eat, good health, stable home. To this, we might add the essential of satisfying work.

What we can easily overlook are the manifold comforts which cushion the main structure of our lives, but are often taken for granted: the small kindnesses of friends and neighbours, the grace and devotion of domestic pets, the ''grapevine'' care of a community, the sheer beauty of simple, everyday things. David Hill's inner eye has seen and appreciated many of these.

Reading this book is like stopping to talk to a friend on a pleasant afternoon. You go on your way afterwards looking forward to the next conversation.

June Shepherd
Crossways
Redgrave

August 1990

LOT 1
A Living in the Past

"Lot number one" called the auctioneer, "three chairs", "Hip, hip, hurray" shouted the inevitable wit amid groans and cheers and the sale was under way.

"Old jokes are the best" was one of many favourite sayings of my mother-in-law. I hadn't intended introducing her so early in the story but having done so I may as well give her pride of place. Other members of the family will appear in due course.

It's a tuppenny cheese-cake to a £5 note that you don't know where Bruisyard is. My wife's grandmother came from there; she was a farmer's wife. We went there recently to do some ancestor hunting in the churchyard.

If you were to search all Suffolk, I don't think that you could find a more delightful place. It is a charming rural enclave, hardly touched, one feels, by the 20th century.

There are small enclosed meadows with high hedges, wandering lanes, unbridged fords and even a vineyard to visit before coming to the church. This small, round-towered building stands at the head of a lime walk on a slight hill above the lush valley. The family graves are clustered around the southern porch.

I knew my wife's grandmother some time before I met my wife. I had driven her Armstrong-Siddeley at one period when she was without a chauffeur – it was like driving a tank. I remember her for her expression, "It's no use getting old if you don't get artful."

We also had a common aunt; a more accurate than flattering description. That situation had come about when an uncle of mine had married one of my wife's aunts. This, you may note, is quite in order according to the Table of Kindred and Affinity.

In addition to being quite in order, it had the pleasant advantage of our two families being fairly well acquainted, so that when the two of us finally came together we immediately had a lot in common and were also saved a great deal of having "to meet the family".

For a late Victorian, my mother-in-law had a notably racy turn of speech and a strong addiction to the use of slang. It was quite easy to

7

detect the source of some expressions which she habitually used. Her brother was a captain in the merchant marine and her Scottish grandfather the captain of a whaler.

From these two derived a whole compass of salty expressions. "A new outfit from truck to keel," or "Always had his back teeth awash" are sufficient illustration.

There are equally clear indications of other connections, with Malaya, Anglo-India and other outposts of Empire in references to "tiffin" and more frequently to "chota pegs".

Although mother-in-law was most certainly no chowpork, there was enough residual farmer's wife for her to be well versed in the East Anglian vernacular.

In addition to all this, she delighted in a little namedropping and expressions such as, "Doesn't come from 'our' side of the family, dear"; and "Not quite one of us", were entirely to be expected.

On this aspect, I like to recall her statement, "Our milk comes from Lord Rayleigh's farm", and the 'sotto voce' rejoinder from another member of the family, "And not everyone is privileged to drink the milk of the nobility".

Some expressions came strangely from the lips of a former part-convent educated girl. "As much chance as a snowball in hell", or "The biggest liar God ever put breath into", were routine observations.

It was perhaps in the field of personal assessments that her phraseology excelled. Unfortunate objects of her pithy comment were likely to be castigated as being "Daft as a halfpenny watch", have "legs like a billiard table", "hair like a pound of candles" and "not know A from a bull's foot".

I don't seem to recall any remarks which were both colourful and complimentary.

Once she had got over the fact that I was "in trade", mother-in-law was always all right with me. One mild reproof I recall occurred when I foolishly mentioned that I could hear rather better with one ear than the other. She looked me straight in the eye and said, "My boys are perfect".

In the course of time she conferred this accolade upon her granddaughters but we males always came off second best.

I bought those three chairs at the auction. Odd trio that they were, they went into our barn to join the motley collection from which we were able from time to time to match with a set of six or more. But I am getting ahead of myself and must go back to explain how it came about that my wife and I were buying and selling chairs.

Quite recently I was asked, "How did you get into selling country antiques?'' A good question for which I had to stop and think for a good answer. It was by accident. We were, as they say, at a crossroads, too early for retirement and not well enough placed financially even to consider that road. My previous job had come to an end and a decision had to be made.

After being self-employed for nearly all my working life to that point, I thought that it would be rather a good idea to become an employee for the next ten years or so; to be somebody else's worry and perhaps even qualify for an occupational pension at the end of it. I did all those things which people do when looking for a job. I wrote numerous applications and attended some entertaining interviews. There was some difficulty at first as I was more used to being the interviewer than the interviewee. There was a tendency for wires to become crossed.

I turned down two offers. One would have been an interesting job for about twelve months or so but, I judged, would then have started to drive me mad. The other involved what I consider to be unsocial hours and the almost inevitable consumption of more beer than I could contemplate.

It soon became clear that not too many employers were going to be interested in me at my age so then my wife and I started applying for joint positions. If my solo interviews were entertaining then our joint ventures were hilarious. Again we turned down two offers. We could just about visualise ourselves as custodians of a stately home, open to the public, and found out in the nick of time that we were expected to do all the cleaning – at least my wife was, my chief preoccupations would have been looking after the peacocks and two oil-fired boilers. Our second escape was from becoming 'in loco parentis' to thirty female Virginian exchange students at Reading University. I thought that I might have enjoyed that but my wife couldn't face the thought of cooking a Thanksgiving dinner for thirty.

All this time our sister-in-law had been urging us to go into the antiques business. We resisted the idea for some time on the grounds that, unlike her, we knew little about antiques. She promised to help us get started and in the end we decided to give it a whirl. We bought an old forge complete with blacksmith's cottage, a useful range of outbuildings and a stream through the garden.

When we first saw the cottage, the long grass of summer choked the garden and hollyhocks curtained the lattice windows. There was never a moment's doubt that it would be a happy home. A few days after we moved in, there was an auction sale in town – ''450 lots of Antiques and Cottage Furniture and miscellaneous effects, removed from local residences for the convenience of sale''. We went along and bought some furniture more in tune with our new home: a pair of rush seated ladderbacks and a pine table for our kitchen-living room, some elm seated Windsor chairs and one or two oddments which took my wife's fancy, including a small pine chest.

In the all-absorbing process of getting settled in, the pine chest got pushed into the black space under the stairs and forgotten. It was Michaelmas when we moved into the cottage and almost Christmas before we remembered the chest, pulled it out one evening and settled down beside the fire to go through the contents. To say that we came upon treasure would be an exaggeration but we were enthralled by everything, right down to the paper lining the bottom. Statelier homes possess their muniment room with well-documented records of all things pertaining to the estate. We had unwittingly bought our own muniment; a commentary on our cottage and sufficient material to form a picture of its principal inhabitant. We had in fact bought a box which had belonged to the methodical and lately departed Miss Finch.

"Oh yes!" they had said at the village shop in answer to our enquiries, "Miss Finch lived alone with her parrot. She had a bomb in her thatch". In our ignorance we took this to mean that she had been in a state of mental confusion. Nothing could have been further from the truth. The contents of that little pine chest illustrated a well-ordered existence and a methodical mind.

It would, I suppose, be possible to sort all the items from that box into two piles – one relating to the cottage and one to Miss Finch. But that would be a pity as the two were mutually dependent. First to hold our attention was one of those wire spikes on which receipted bills are impaled. The last one to be spiked was for "7lbs Parrot food, 14lbs Bird sand, 1 pkt. Tonic Grit". The absurd thought arose that this was how Miss Finch had sustained herself. Receipted bird food bills were not the only regular items on the spike. Rates had been paid with metronome regularity and Broadcasting Receiver Licences marked the passing years. In 1950, "Slight repairs to roof" had cost £1 5s 4d – a trifle compared with the 12 guineas for repairs to exterior plaster 20 years earlier, and this too had been dwarfed by the bill which we had just paid for similar items.

A cutting from the "Advertiser" enlightened us in the matter of a bomb in her thatch. It was during those "slight repairs to roof" that a large anti-personnel bomb had been discovered and ultimately removed by the disposal squad from Colchester. If Miss Finch had been regular with her payments, her regularity had been matched by "the Man from the Pru". One could easily believe that it had been possible to tell not only the date but probably the time of day marked by his

10

monthly arrival to collect four shillings and to put his initials in the growing pile of Premium Receipt Books. A "Notice of Post War Credits" turned up as a reminder that great events had been happening beyond the peace of this little cottage and the well-regulated life within it. So, too, did a folded copy of the "News of the World" dated 17th June, 1917 – "Zeppelin destroyed over East Coast" reads one headline. Beecham's pills, we noted, were still worth a guinea a box!

The carefully kept documents in the pine box were at odds with the heterogenous jumble of other objects. We suspected that whoever was deputed to tidy up the cottage before the sale had thrown in the contents of other containers. Spread out on a table, they reminded us of a giant contest of Kim's Game. There were a number of useful items such as a darning mushroom, crochet hooks, rag rug-making tools, bodkins, nail files and scissors. A tin which had originally contained "Brampton Hospital Formula Chest and Lung Lozenges" now contained every size of pin. Items less useful included broken spectacles, odd buttons in profusion, Christmas seals stuck in wads, empty cotton reels, a tangled web of perished elastic and some odd suspender clips – all of them like displaced persons drifting around until forgotten.

From the bottom of the box we extracted a copy of the "Sunday People" dated 17th October, 1897. There was news of a cat show at the Crystal Palace and a strangely familiar account of strikes and ferment in the engineering industry. We feel sure that Miss Finch would have approved of the first item only, but the paper was issued two months before her birth on 7th December, 1897, when the cottage was already 200 years old. The cottage has, of course, had other inhabitants but they are shadowy figures. We sometimes felt that we were only privileged guests and that one day Miss Finch might return. If that was possible, the hanging flower basket would have to come off the hook quickly to make way for the parrot's cage and the shameful muddle of papers on my desk would need to be swept aside. I think she would have liked the new kitchen and would certainly have approved of the just-completed thatch.

The name of our new home, "Old Forge Cottage" might well have been the only reminder of a once thriving business. In fact we worked hard to ensure that a business still prospered, but of rather a different nature. This difference of nature was almost our undoing. We were advised that planning permission would be required for change of use. "But," I protested, "there has been a workshop here of one sort and another for at least three hundred years."

"Aha!" replied the bureaucrats, "A fig for the past three hundred, it's the last seven years we are interested in."

11

The Old Forge.

So that little thing, like the nail from the horse's shoe, almost changed the course of our lives and nearly frustrated our endeavours before they began. Fortunately good sense prevailed and we were able to save a listed building from the decay of neglect and disuse.

Picture, if you can, this idyllic rural setting right on the fringe of Constable country. The artist himself was adept at idealizing Suffolk cottages and he certainly started off with very promising material. Our cottage had the advantages of age; a softening of outline, irregularity of shape; a mellowness which is neither quickly nor easily achieved. Even more important to us was what the agent referred to as ''the range of outbuildings''. These included a miniature barn, a minute (and condemned) cottage and the former smithy.

It would have given us enormous pleasure if we had found inside the smithy at least the basic hardware of the trade. We found only two items: the bellows, six feet long and mighty impressive but bereft of their levers and cow's horn handgrip, and a notably solid workbench of blackened oak, strapped to wall and floor by iron bands, toilworn and crusted with nails.

Of the hearth itself there was nothing but the chimney, no canopy remained. It was clear that even when in position it had often proved inadequate to take away all the smoke produced in the pit. There was a pump but no water-trough, no tools or vice and, most conspicuous in their absence, neither anvil nor the massive block of wood on which it was set to give it spring.

But there was plenty of soot and grime. The cobwebs were the black lace of deepest mourning which when swept away revealed the beams and rafters kippered beneath the thatch.

Our son William joined us at this point – ''just to help you get started''. Looking back to those early days I do not believe that we would ever have got started without him.

We added to the dust by removing a partition wall. William and I gave it a few exploratory taps with our hammers. It was wattle and daub. We thought that we would have it cleared by lunch-time but we were still working at it by the evening. The hazel rods were iron hard, preserved within their casing of lime mortar.

Two tons was our estimate of the dirt and rubble which we removed from the smithy and used for the basis of a car park. We swept and shovelled and we swept again. A craftsman made and fitted some windows for us while we repaired the thatch. Then we sluiced right through the started painting.

We created a studio/workshop of considerable charm, a pleasant place in which to work, a setting stimulating to the imagination and redolent of the past. Although all the trappings of the former trade were missing (with the noble exceptions of bench and bellows), the form and feel of the building remained, so that it was easily peopled from the past in the mind's eye.

Even more delightful was that some of these figments of the imagination came alive!

Our butcher came in to see us working. "I've not been in here since I brought a horse to be shod. Her name was Myrtle, I know where one of her shoes lay." He brought it the following week; a great soup-plate of a shoe. We nailed it to the door to remind the Devil that St. Dunstan had extracted from him a promise never again to enter a building where a horseshoe is displayed.

Two neighbours came in with similar stories to tell and a third told us of the part he used to play helping both smith and wheelwright. We stopped work and searched for the old tyre ring, but realignment of the road had altered the lie of the land as well as cutting fourteen feet off the travus where the horses waited to be shod.

Then one afternoon the principle character of this bygone tableau walked in and joined us for a cup of tea. At last we were going to learn all the missing details and have a firsthand account of working in the old forge. But the former Smith was a quite, gentle man, thoroughly steeped in our East Anglian habit of reticence and understatement.

How long was it since he last shoed a horse?

"Ah! Quite some time."

Happily his wife was less reticent. When we went over to the cottage she evidently felt quite at home again. She produced some photographs of the cottage, the pub, and the brook. These, together with an aerial view which we had, clearly showed the more recent changes which had taken place in this little corner of Suffolk. There have, I suspect, been more of these during the past hundred years or less than in all the rest of the time since the Roman Legions forded the stream at this point. The line of the Roman road from Colchester to the settlement at Ixworth is still clear to be seen – it is the details which have been altered.

The railway has come and gone, leaving footpaths and bridleways between neighbouring hamlets. Like the forge itself, the mill over the road has lost its real purpose in life and also like the forge there are no records of its origins.

The airfield up on the hill has not all returned to agricultural use – its place in history is recorded in "Suffolk Summer" by the late John Appleby of the U.S.A.

Almost everywhere around those glorious hedgerows have been uprooted; no longer needed to confine huge flocks of Suffolk sheep, they have become obstacles to mechanised progress.

We talked of these things over a cup of tea and I was told about other features now missing from the life of the hamlet: the wheelwright's shop, the village store and, of course, the school. This latter, we agreed, may well be revived as a sensible alternative to the coaches which daily and expensively transport the children to and from more distant institutions.

Strangely enough, although I met the last smith to work in the forge, I seem to know more of his predecessor. From chance remarks I have built up a picture of Mr. Goldsmith at work in the smithy.

"Twenty stone he were and his wife only two stone short of that. He was a big man with it and it was some effort for him to get down and lift a horse's foot."

That he was a fine craftsment has never been disputed. More than one of our new-found friends and neighbours recalled the skill with which he forged and fixed shoes on the horses which they brought to him.

"When I was a boy I lived up over the hill. I used to bring horses to the forge on my way to school. When they were ready they were taken over the road. Mr. Ruffle let them stand there until I came out of school and took them home."

"The old boys from the farms came in for a bit of shelter and warmth when it was wet and windy. It was better than reading any newspaper. We heard what was going on and some pretty strong opinions too."

"Old Goldsmith would tolerate us all for a time then he'd get fed up and say 'Go yew on the lot of yew and leave me in peace'."

"He wasn't one to argue with, what with his size and he could show a slice of temper when he got riled, but he was generally very quiet and gentle with horses. He had one nasty trick with them though if one got him on the raw. Out under the travus the roof beams were very low. If he gave the offending horse a sharp jab it would rear up and hit its head on solid oak. 'That will take the wickedness out of him' he said."

"There were several feet more of that travus before the road was altered. It reached out low to the edge of the lane. The lane ran close by the two cottages and round the corner of the barn."

"He kept a great ole parrot in a cage near the stable door. It was properly educated. It swore something horrible and frightened us boys."

"It was quieter down here in them times. You could hear the sound of hammering in the forge and you could hear the splash and rumble of the mill working. I doubt you couldn't do that now."

"Us boys liked to get in and work the bellows for him. Yes, those are the bellows in the corner but of course they were set up behind the hearth. I can still hear him say 'Keep it steady, boy. Up smart and down gentle.' Those are single acting bellows."

"I suppose he did, but it seemed that he never made a mistake, always striking them nails true so they came through clean to be clinched and smooth on the hoof. He said it was a waste of his time if he cold-shod a horse – it would soon have to come back and be done properly. 'Fact I recall one horse which was cold shod and it hardly got to the top of Cold Hill before it was giving trouble."

"When you worked a pair of horses, it wasn't all that uncommon for one to tread on the other's foot and start a shoe which hadn't been properly fitted and bedded on."

"Goldsmith made all the shoes he used. So far as I know he never had no truck with prefabricated shoes."

"We used to help ourselves to some of Mr. Ruffle's apples from over the road. We cut them up in small pieces and fed them to our horses. It kept their minds off what Mr. Goldsmith was doing. Of course, we ate some of them ourselves."

"I remember seeing the heated tyres being put on the wooden wheels. When we were old enough we were allowed to help. The tyre ring was set in the ground over there between the forge and the brook. It's all been altered now. the main road is nearer this way. The old bridge was closer to the mill and the main road ran up the hill past the Rose and Crown. The forge and the cottages weren't never on the main road really. They were on the lane to Lavenham and the lane was on this side of the brook."

Re-alignment of the main road had caused some confusion as to where the parish boundary now lies. We believed that we lived in Long Melford. Mr. Goldsmith clearly had no doubt that he lived in Alpheton; his delightful printed billhead proclaims it clearly. We found a receipted bill dated September 1925 between the leaves of a leatherbound ledger. It is an account for six months work done for Mr. Smith of Kiln Farm; a detailed list of skill, craft and honest sweat, all for the sum of two pounds, fourteen shillings and three pence. If Mr. Goldsmith had faults, avarice was not among them.

Speaking the other day of this former occupant of the old forge, my neighbour said, "He weren't a bad ole boy." In East Anglia this passes as fairly high praise. If nothing more is said of me when I go, I believe that I will rest easy.

LOT 2
A Girl called Jennifer

"Do you find that the locals accept you?" I was asked by a recent refugee from the Home Counties.

"Well" I replied, "the boot is really on the other foot. I've been an East Anglian for 68 years."

It is true that I have moved around a bit, having now spent about thirty years in each of Norfolk and Suffolk, while living the other few years in odd places such as Essex, Nigeria and India.

My birth certificate states that I was born in West Wymer which has a rather North American flavour but turns out to have been a Sub-District of the County Borough of Norwich. The name has, I fancy, long since disappeared in the face of progress, just like the tin hut at the top of Grove Avenue wherein I was christened. I note from the entry on the back of the certificate that I was issued with a ration book. That at least was a little piece of history which was to be repeated some years later.

What is it that entitles one to belong to a region? Surely not place of birth alone, for it is perfectly possible to be born in Timbuktoo and to be as English as a cricket bat and fiercely regional in allegiance.

My Granddaughters can claim to be East Anglian by birth with at least five generations before them making the same claim. I am less sure of my lineage for more than three generations back though I have long understood that one side of the family came to East Anglia with the Flemish Weavers. That would trace my middle name back to the fourteenth or sixteenth century so I ought to have no trouble with my claim to be an East Anglian.

I ought to have no trouble yet I was surprised when a customer challenged me saying: "You don't sound as if you belong round here."

"That's possibly because I was educated in Surrey" I replied. It was a lucky shot as it turned out that the customer lives in College Road, Epsom. Lucky, because I make no claim to be a Professor Higgins able to recognise precise regional accents or dialects.

We in East Anglia have rich variety in our origins. I have no clear idea who preceded the Iceni — some say it was the Gaels or possibly Iberians. It is said that until quite recently the inhabitants of Brandon

17

contrasted strikingly with the rest of the people in the two counties, having very dark hair and eyes. Certainly the craft of flint knapping has been carried on there ever since pre-historic times. It would be no surprise to find that the last of the knappers had their roots deep in the Stone Age.

So the Romans found a funny old lot when they came and they were followed by the Saxons and Angles who settled and were joined by Norsemen or Danes and of course the Dutch. Between them they evolved the language which has left its early influences in our dialect and on our place names with their -by -ham and -ton suffices.

When my wife and I moved from East Suffolk to North Norfolk I was immediately struck by the difference in the people. There were even facial differences to be noted and more especially a different approach to life.

Our next move took us almost to the border of East Saxony or Essex as they now call it. I did once live South of the river Stour for a year. They laughed at me when I went home and said that I had an Essex accent.

Today our home is near the source of the rivers Waveney and Little Ouse. I live in Suffolk and work in Norfolk. The best of two worlds is how I see it.

My mother was an avid daily reader of the local daily paper so it is quite possible that I was born with the same addiction, and I note that I started my first press cutting collection at the age of nine. Aptly enough the first item is a letter to the Editor under the heading: ''Out of the mouths of babes . . .'' It was written by the late Walter Dearnaley about a rugger match between Town Close House School and Lancing House, played at Lowestoft.

Of course I was one of the 'babes', and I remember the match chiefly on account of the fact that it was just about the only time I ever scored a try. I like to think that this was because of the position in which I consistently played from those days onward, but it might also have been part of my makeup. My Kindergarten mistress, Miss Lincolne, recalls: ''a charming boy, steady and very reliable, whose parents were exceedingly nice people.'' Not brilliant or even clever, but just a steady plodder, and we are not the ones who score tries.

If it is surprising that Miss Lincolne still remembers me, it is natural enough that I remember her. Recently, while in Norwich, I drove along Newmarket Road and saw the For Sale notice up again on number 135. It was there that we first met, for it was then Winton School, which later formed the nucleus of Town Close House. I don't have to drive past the scene to remember those days; many small things can easily recall them, such as hymn tune or a name not spoken for a number of years. It took me nearly fifty years to learn Miss Lincolne's christian name. Indeed who would ever have suspected that a presiding deity, however benevolent, had anything so frivolous as a christian name and certainly not one so charming as Lucilla.

At the first notes of "There is a green hill far away . . ." I can see her, entirely in command of any situation, standing at the end of the long wooden hut which formed our classroom. It may not have been as long as memory makes it, but certainly there were wooden flap tables along both sides to supplement the places in the centre. The flaps were held up by chains which were not quite strong enough for the job, or perhaps we were over rough with them.

On one side of the room there were two tortoise stoves which either smoked very badly and gave insufficient heat or got red hot. When we sharpened our pencils on the top of a hot stove there was a delicious smell of smouldering cedarwood.

I can see very clearly the copy books which we filled once we had passed the stage of writing over the letters with tracing paper. It wasn't just the flowing Palace Script which we learnt, but the bon mots themselves: "Manners Maketh Man", or "Silence is Golden". (Perhaps I am wrong about that one, it was a Mr Golden who taught us arithmetic later on in the more senior forms).

It was George who came and poured coke into the tortoise stoves and knew about all things practical such as blowing up footballs and fixing bicycles. In his case I never knew his surname. One of his most popular activities was operating the film projector. This was housed in a metal booth which stood in another wooden annex to the main house. We were shown educational films with a ration of cartoons which was increased at the end of term showing. They were of course silent films, which require a greater degree of audience participation.

At the back end of our kindergarten classroom there was a sand table in which I see depicted strange biblical scenes; products of curious combinations of geography and scripture, of sand, plasticine and paper models. There was also a Nature Table from which my clearest recollection is that of a broad bean growing impaled on a hat pin and supplied with moisture from damp cotton wool in the bottom of the jar. We marked the growth of its shoot each week on a paper scale and drew pictures to record progress. Also stowed at that end of the room was a wooden box horse and springboard on which we were later introduced to the beginnings of gymnastics.

My sister is also an 'old boy' of the school, which was co-educational until about the time I went there; I see from a photograph in which she

19

appears that in those earlier days they also had grass in the playground. In my time it had become smooth hard-packed earth; a good enough surface for Physical Training and impromptu games and an excellent one for 'doing skids' on bicycles. If it is ungallant of me to have mentioned that I am younger than my sister, I must add that Miss Lincolne, who moved to Cambridge, remembered her as "older than David, and clever!"

I received one of my sister's newsy letters the other day: "I enjoyed your article last week", wrote my sister. "Of course it was all about nothing as usual, but it was just like you." Not high praise, but I appreciated it, for in truth, almost any comment is better than none. It is impossible to regard one's own literary creations in an entirely dispassionate light. Even a work of fiction contains so much of oneself that it is easy to become over-protective. A rejection slip, for example, however kindly phrased, is like criticism of one's children; however well justified it is hard to take.

I have an interesting collection of these slips. Some of them are beautifully illustrated to soften their impact. They appear to range from curt printed items to hand-written messages. The first time I received one of the latter, I thought how nice and civil it was to have so personal a communication. I now have three of these identical "hand written" rejections and realise that I was deceived by a printer's art.

If there is little honour to be found near home, encouragement, when it comes, is more often from further afield. It is this follow-up and correspondence resulting from articles which gives me so much pleasure.

One most charming letter came from an octogenarian. It had been prompted by a piece about the river Yare, where I played as a boy. He should have written the article himself for he had a fund of interesting stories including the rescue by horse and cart of the miller marooned by flood water in Cringleford Mill.

I also accepted the invitation of an old friend who wrote: "We still live in the same place which you mentioned, and have nearly reached the half century here. We still have a boat, so if you have time to squander and would like to voyage as of yore, the said boat is at your disposal." A sorry footnote to the happy day which ensued was that soon afterwards the boat was stolen.

A less likely letter came one day from Croydon. My correspondent had picked up a reference to the Graf Zepplin, which I had photographed from the cliffs at Mundesley. Consequently this photo is now to be seen as an illustration in "East Anglia 1939" by Douglas Brown. It was also instrumental in my meeting the author.

As well as helping to make new friends, sometimes old friendships have been revitalised. Welcome letters have come from such people as the retired Civil Engineer whom I had quoted as starting an after dinner speech with the words, "Most people's troubles are over when they pull the chain — that is when ours begin." Or the ex-R.A.F. Pilot who nearly landed his Sunderland flying boat on a tarmac runway, switched successfully to the river Orwell and then stepped out into the water, saying, "That was a near thing, chaps!"

Occasionally, an alert correspondent is kind enough to draw my attention to errors of fact. For these I am always grateful. There is an ever present danger that people will believe something simply because they see it in print. I didn't even need to have been a printer to be aware of this fallacy.

My sister mentioned having been shopping in Elm Hill, the scene of some of my most enduring childhood memories.

About halfway down the hill there is a coaching entrance. Just inside, on the left, is a doorway and a flight of stairs which leads up to a large room where, many years ago, I attended dancing classes. I have never forgotten the experience.

Looking back on all the various classes which I have attended, I am quite surprised at the range of them. I realise, too, that at one point, there was a sort of watershed. The ones which I was obliged to attend were all up-hill work. Thereafter, when I made my own choices and went to classes voluntarily, work became a pleasure.

Of course, the first portion of my education included school, which can be passed over quickly. Then came technical and managerial education, fulltime and evening classes. I hadn't long emerged from that lot when along came the Army with an almost endless succession of courses and classes.

There were useless subjects, such as chemical warfare, useful ones like map-reading and interpretation of aerial photography, interesting subjects such as gunnery or the use of explosives, and others to which I will append no adjectives, which included parachute training and unarmed combat.

When I left the Army, I went on a Ministry of Labour Resettlement course and that was really the turning point. From then on I was more or less in charge of my own life. I couldn't then blame anyone if I subsequently found myself in a class which was less than entertaining.

For reasons which now elude me, I signed on for classes in Public Speaking. A masochistic choice it now seems to me. At the time I am sure that I was encouraged by those advertisements which promised that after such a course, the other members of the Board would be convinced by my arguments when I got to my feet and spoke. I even remember the name of our charming instructor and her classes were great fun. They included such matters as the duties of a chairman and a session or two on the art of proposing a vote of thanks. Even if I never swayed a Board Meeting with my eloquence, at least I learned about a lot of pitfalls to be avoided.

A quite different enthusiasm led me to become a student of East Anglian Geology. Our W.E.A. course was made up of sessions in the lecture room alternating with field expeditions. We searched diligently for marine fossils, examined glacial moraines around Sheringham, studied flints in Breckland, chalk deposits at Weybourne, cannon-shot gravel on Mousehold and paramoudra on the beach of East Runton. There was something called a Glacial Erratic which now eludes me and Coralline Crag, or perhaps that was one of the female students.

No, I do now remember Coralline.

Our meeting place was to be Chillesford Church, near Orford. It took me a long time to get there by way of a trail which started in that W.E.A. lecture room.

One day, following a field expedition, a friend of mine asked, ''What on earth were you lot doing at Brameton last night?''

It was easy to understand why our appearance had baffled her. As our group had assembled to board our coach anyone watching us might well have been puzzled to assess our common denominator. Our ages ranged from 17 to 70 and our choice of garb was just as disparate. When my friend saw us, we were making a sortie to examine marine deposits rich in fossils.

If I have forgotten much that we were told in the classroom, I have remembered well those expeditions. They were the illustrations in the text — always more memorable than mere words. The specimens which we collected were details from those illustrations; small fragments which go together to make the wonderful diversity and beauty of East Anglia.

We visited Thorpe Pits in that area where the Yare comes through the chalk barrier into the coastal plain. Chalk from these pits was carried by wherries to such places as the cement works powered by the great windmill at Berney Arms, to lime kilns and to farms when marl was widely used as top dressing.

Although we searched diligently, we made no such find as the skeleton of a mastodon which was once uncovered at Horstead pits. Don't ask where those bones now lie, for, regrettably, before the scientists arrived, the bones had been burnt with the chalk and reduced to lime.

The chalk at Weybourne, which forms the low cliff, and ends so abruptly where the shingle bank begins, has a different nature. This is "reworked chalk", which was deposited in the normal manner, then churned up and redeposited by movement of the Earth.

It follows quite naturally that this area of geological interest is also one of great beauty. Those strange hills and ridges, set back from the present coastline, are parts of a terminal moraine; the dross and rubble pushed there by great glaciers coming down from the north east.

Flints, which one always associates with chalk, are very much part of our local scene. I love the familiar blend of grey flint with mellow red brick or imported dressed stone; our uniquely beautiful round-towered churches; whole villages or isolated cottages. My heart lifts as I see the first of these in Breckland, knowing that my homeward journey is nearly done.

Of course we went to Brandon to visit Grimes Graves; probably the most anicent "industrial estate" in the whole country, but I will not digress into flint knapping, only recalling that this stratum form of flint is different from our seashore and river washed variety. A most striking example of the latter is to be found in the cannon-shot gravel of Mousehold.

We paused only briefly in Lakenheath to look at the clunch buildings in the yard of the Bell. This is a remarkably serviceable material providing that it is looked after in much the same way as clay-lump, that is to say, the tops of all such walls need to be well sheltered by a good overhanging roof, and to be well drained at the foot.

I could perhaps at this point tell a story about my old army friend, George. We were seasick together on troopships and suffered various other adversities, all of which served as mortar to bond the bricks of our friendship.

We sat together one summer's day drinking beer. George got to talking about an uncle's farm on which he often stayed as a boy. "Part of this farm is 'listed' for its geological interest," said George. "This particular part is known as Potterscrouch Chalk Pit. One of the few places where Paramoudra are to be found."

"These large flints", said George, "are barrel-shaped, with hollow tubular centres and are found standing upright in the chalk."

"They range in size", he continued, "up to two feet high and one foot diameter."

George told me that the name was probably introduced from Northern Ireland and could have derived from the Erse word "Padhramoudhras", meaning "Ugly Paddied".

When he stopped to sup his beer, I was able to say, "We call them

Potstones in East Anglia. We have got one at the corner of our walled garden. It came from the low tide line on the beach at East Runton''.

''Well,'' said George, ''most people don't know what I'm talking about, let alone have one.''

All of which brings me at last to Chillesford. You will, of course, have known all along that Coralline, although of East Anglian extraction and of considerable beauty, was not a tremulous lover waiting impatiently at the lych-gate, but is the rare local building stone. The church tower at Chillesford provides the only considerable example of Coralline Crag to be found. A rare beauty indeed.

The autumn my wife signed up for colloquial French I got immersed in Rushwork. I remember leaving her at the Secondary Modern School and driving to the Junior School for my own class. In five minutes, I was back; we had both gone to the wrong schools. She was inclined to be indignant. ''Fancy being sent to the wrong school at my age!''

''Good evening, Mr Hill'', said my new Instructor, consulting her list. ''There can't be any doubt who you are.'' Indeed there couldn't, for there I was, the only thorn among the roses of the Rushwork Class. They accepted me as an equal.

I can still quote from the Handbook of Crafts which states that ''Rush chair seating is easy to learn. Anyone reasonably competent with handwork would be able to seat a chair satisfactorily''. I don't quarrel with that statement.

Some years later, I embarked on a natural sequel to rush-seating and signed for Upholstery. What charming students they were. We met with our chairs one afternoon each week. Like dogs and their owners, there were notable affinities in shape and general appearances.

You may notice that all my forays into fun-time education have been on the practical rather than the academic side. I have also avoided such subjects as Cookery and Flower Arranging which I can pick up secondhand. There have been one or two failures but who wants to hear about them?

Every class has its special memories, the successes, the failures, laughter and achievements. None more vivid than thoughts of the sheer agony, the acute sweaty-palmed embarrassment of the Dancing Class, only made bearable by a girl called Jennifer.

LOT 3
Setting the Scene

One of our first visitors after my wife and I moved into the Old Forge was a friend whom we had not seen for some years. He got out of his car, took one look and said, ''This must be a dream come true.'' He was of course absolutely right. Our thatched cottage in its own half acre with mature fruit trees embodied most of the elements of a townsman's dream of a place in the country 'away from the madding crowd'. I should perhaps mention that it also concealed behind its smiling welcome most of his fears about such things as vermin in the roof, erratic public services and trouble with drains. None of these features was new to us. The novelty of our new home was the swift flowing stream which forms part of the boundary of the property. It was this which had captured our hearts.

Quite apart from all its guests and fellow travellers, a stream such as the Chad Brook has a life of its own; it is a living changing thing with character and many changing moods. In the time that we lived beside it we saw it change from a thin clear trickle to a surging turgid torrent and almost as quickly back to a lively stream of champagne brilliance.

It has a voice which ranges from almost silent stealth through tinkle and gurgle to something near to sullen rage of flood; a gamut of sound to match each change of mood.

All these we saw and heard from my workshop, from our living-room or late and early from our bedroom window, and as we watched the seasons change we also saw that we were not the only ones to appreciate our little brook. Riparian owners we were, with exclusive fishing rights from our bank to the centre of the stream but clearly Kingfisher and Heron care nothing for such legal niceties. No stickleback is safe from these fisherman.

We first saw the Kingfisher as a streak of blue between the willows and later disappearing beneath the bridge. It was not until the leaves fell from the willows that we could watch him fishing. One morning in November there he was, his plumage gleaming in the winter sunshine as he perched low over the water. Kingfishers seem to have a natural affinity with places of beauty and enchantment – no wonder they were surrounded by myths of the halcyon days. This one was so artistically framed by the sweeping willow wands that no artist could have improved on the composition of which he formed the focal point.

It turned out to be one of his regular fishing perches. On that first morning we watched him make seven forays. Four times he emerged from the water with a fish. On these occasions he went to a second perch at the foot of the same willow. Each time he made sure that his catch was dead by shaking it and tapping on the branch. Then he tossed it up to swallow it headfirst before returning to his fishing perch. There he waited, poised very still and upright with his tail straight down and head on one side in a contemplative attitude.

Our sightings of the Heron were usually less intimate. Most days we saw him morning and evening as we exercised the dog along the track beside the stream. He would rise some distance ahead of us and heave himself rather laboriously to a safe distance from where he usually watched us pass or sometimes he circled round us and heaved upstream in search of solitude. The happiest exceptions to this routine were when we could watch him emerge from the shadows below the bridge and walk sedately along the imaginary line which forms our boundary, pausing from time to time to observe for long suspended moments and stabbing swiftly with his lethal bill.

All through summer the first sound I heard each morning was the call of a moorhen. I was delighted to be able to watch the family party from my workshop. An occasional handful of grain was sufficient to bring them up the bank to feed and squabble a few feet from the window. She was a good mother, and among other things she kept a sharp look-out for the Heron, especially while her chicks were small enough to present him with a variation to his diet. Mallard and Teal have also figured among our visitors from the brook, and a Muscovy called Tom whose wandering was strictly unauthorised and he was soon collected by his owner.

But, if like Shakespeare's Olivia, I ''give out diverse schedules'' of the beauties of our brook, and even ''if every particle be labelled'', still I would fail to draw its character. Like the quicksilver it so often imitates, it is difficult to pin down. It changes with day and season. In winter it is sometime aloof; mobile while all else is gripped in frost. It is generous and bountiful in spring, giving new life to all who draw on it. In summer it is cool and refreshing when all else turns to dust. Autumn is the least well defined of the four seasons and so too is the character of our stream at that time.

For most of its course down the valley the Chad Brook is deep down in the cutting which it has created for itself. By the time autumn comes rank vegetation has filled its course from bank to bank. The brook makes no objection but flows gently on 'half hidden from the eye'. As soon as the heavy rains come the brook re-asserts itself as if it had been biding its time, knowing that when it returned to a season of strength it would sweep away all impediments.

I never saw the flowing waters stilled by frost. We walked its rock-hard banks with a great variety of spoor set hard as evidence of nocturnal visitors we never saw. Muntjak and their young left their slot in fair numbers. Otters too, no doubt hard pressed for a meal, left evidence of their maraudings beyond the confines of the brook.

Throughout the seasons the Chad Brook adds its waters to the River Stour, passing Gainsborough's birthplace and flowing on through Constable country. I mention this with a touch of envy for perhaps it takes an artist to portray this beauty which captured our hearts.

To an East Anglian it should have come as no surprise to look out of our windows and see water and willows. The surprise for me was the realization that the willows which I saw were mine. Not so the waters of the Brook for I understand that the running water of a natural stream is owned by no one until it is impounded. But I was a riparian owner and a proud one even though I had rather hazy knowledge of just what that meant.

The Brook.

27

I hesitated to enquire too deeply into the exact extent of my rights as I felt sure that in this bureaucratic age many ancient and natural rights would have been whittled away by a succession of misguided and interfering Acts.

I am surprised that when we were buying the property our agent made no mention of the stream. The particulars of sale might well have carried a note to the effect that 'sporting rights are in hand'. Perhaps he thought that too much emphasis on the nearness of the stream would give rise to thoughts of flooding or excessive dampness. I am happy to record that neither of these was the case. The water was NOT "all slippy sloppy in the larder and in the back passage".

Beyond the woods our stream crossed and re-crossed the course of the old railway before feeding the ornamental waters of Melford Hall and passing under the main road to join the Stour.

We spent most of one Bank Holiday along the valley trying to find a thatcher who would come and do some repairs on our thatch. You might think that a public holiday was a curious time to choose for such a mission but we thought that it would give us the best chance to find these elusive craftsman at home or perhaps at their local pubs. It was a thoroughly enjoyable but totally unproductive day. The consensus of answers to our enquiries was, "Well now, I would have liked to have helped you but I haven't done any thatching for four or five years. Can't get the straw, you know, these combine harvesters make a nonsense of it".

So there we were at the end of a long but happy day still with a gaping hole in our roof where a chimney stack had been and no prospect of expert help in the foreseeable future. Do-it-yourself has thrust itself upon me in many forms but I confess that I had shied away from the thought of becoming my own thatcher.

However, needs must etc. so in my equally new role of riparian owner I pulled on my boots and descended below the willows to the plashy fringes of the brook. It took only a few minutes to cut a couple of good bundles of sedge. We stuffed the rectangular hole with about three-quarters of a bale of straw — mutilated despised combine harvester variety — but by happy chance compressed to almost exactly the right dimensions for the job.

Then we capped it with the sedge, combing it, easing it into position and pegging it down over the ridge with split willow strips and broaches cut from the hedge. The crowning moment of pleasure was provided by the visiting carpenter: ''I can see that you've done that before,'' he said, and he was wrong, but I had spent some time during a long hot summer watching Joe Stiff, a master craftsman at work on a cottage at Twinstead. I hoped that when he came to do the job properly he would not be too scornfull of our efforts.

It was not in the event Joe Stiff who came to re-thatch the roof of the forge. Another Master Thatcher who I will call Steven and his apprentice Ron arrived to transform the shaggy looking building into one of well groomed neatness worthy of its Grade II listing.

I had taken my typewriter over to the summerhouse to settle down to work with a deadline looming in the none too distant future. I thought that I had a good workable timetable with its objective comfortably in reach. But I hadn't reckoned on Steven turning up.

He and Ron arrived in a well laden truck just as I was collecting my thoughts. It would have been churlish of me not to have stopped work to greet them and just as bad not to have given a hand unloading the great pile of Norfolk reeds. We stacked them on what we laughingly called the lawn. In reality it was some rough grass which sloped down to the stream and was kept short by Harry and Hilda, a pair of Canada geese to whom I will introduce you later.

Harry and Hilda quickly accepted Steven as a friend but never really trusted Ron so that a state of mutual wariness existed all the time he was with us.

The bundles of reed were pleasant to handle. They had a scent somewhere between new-mown hay and mudflats at low tide. It was eleven o'clock before I got back to my typewriter and even then I found it hard to concentrate as Steven and Ron set up their ladders and proceeded to strip the old thatch. In a very short time the place was a shambles.

As work progressed there were many moments of magic. Up on his sloping ladder Seven caught the yealms as Ron swung them easily to his hand. In all their actions they exercised that economy of movement which so often distinguishes the craftsman from the over enthusiastic amateur. They achieved this transfer of bundles with precision of Olympic relay runners passing the baton. For a few seconds Steven would have two bundles under his left hand as he positioned them. Then, as he worked at them with his legget, they were bundles no more and lost their identity. They merged with their predecessors to form the thatch which seemed almost to grow from his hands, spreading protectively over the rough wooden battens and roof timbers.

Each morning we all stopped work for a cup of tea at about 10 o'clock and with little encouragement Steven would talk about his trade. He

The Thatcher.

was a mine of information and such a good raconteur that he made our tea breaks something to look forward to. It was always hard to get back to work.

Each time Steven worked up to the ridge I could see the feathery heads of the reeds as he slapped and coaxed the yealms into position. The third time was too much for me. I had to go round to the front to see what it looked like. I couldn't miss watching as he worked his way round the chimney stack and then filled in the short pieces between there and the gable. Next thing I knew it was lunch time.

I would have gone straight back to my typewriter afterwards but Steven and Ron were preparing the thick straw rope to lay along the ridge before starting the capping. I badly wanted to see how the capping was done so I hung around a bit and didn't start writing again until it was almost time for tea.

The most magical moment in all creative work is when the craftsman puts the final touch and the job is suddenly whole and complete. It was a race on that sunny Tuesday afternoon between Steven and me. I sternly resisted all temptation to go and watch him doing his final pat and trim, but I couldn't help glancing out of the window from time to time. Steven was trimming the ridge. As he moved his ladder the shaggy capping of the ridge was transformed to a simple, beautiful line of scallops and points.

While Steven moved along steadily towards completion I floundered to a finish. At last I was there. I clipped the pages together and walked round the corner of the cottage just as Steven and Ron swung the long ladder away and lowered it to the ground. 'Well,' said Steven, 'there she is. I'll leave you to tidy up round the garden. I reckon my time is more valuable than what yours is.' I'm sure that he was right. His masterpiece will mellow and ensure for perhaps 40 years; a thing of beauty which will keep out the cold in winter and give cool protection in the heat of the summer. The fruits of my labours can at best give no more than passing pleasure.

As usual, Harry and Hilda had the last word. With necks outstretched and heads lowered they pursued the departing truck to the end of the lane and clearly thought they had achieved a notable victory.

It must be admitted that we spent quite a lot of time looking out of the window in our workshop, watching the happenings down in the stream below the willows. William was the first to see the snake. It was swimming strongly towards us, head well clear of the water, its body forming a sinuous ripple. It came over to the point where our surface water drains into the stream, foraged around for a few moments and then, as if sensing danger, went swiftly back over the water and disappeared among the lush greenery.

The whole incident was over in two or three silent minutes and we were not able to identify it certainly as either grass snake or adder.

I have a book entitled "A Guide to Country Living" to which I often refer when I have an estate management type of problem. It offers information in question and answer form. The only offering under the heading of snakes is as follows:-

"Q. Is there a cure for getting rid of adders (snakes)?

A. The only thing is to find out where they are breeding (probably on a sunny bank), and kill the lot, young and old, by gas, if you have any, such as was used in the destroying of rabbits, or else with gunshot."

This gives me a splendid picture of a peppery old Admiral, left over from the British Empire, but adds little to my knowledge of snakes.

A very widespread revulsion from snakes is largely based on ignorance and undoubtedly dates back to the Garden of Eden. Venomous or not, they are customarily associated with evil, and killed as a matter of course in the manner of my peppery old Admiral, or more often, by a swift blow with a stick.

For our own safety and peace of mind we ought to be able to identify and differentiate between harmless grass snakes and poisonous adders (or vipers vile), for they are the only two species wild in this country.

Size is the first guide. The adder rarely exceeds two feet in length. Any in excess of this, and they can be as much as three or four feet along, are harmless grass snakes. These latter may make gestures of attack, but at the very worst will only eject a foul smelling liquid.

If, however, a snake is seen to be less than two feet long, its colour provides a means of distinguishing between the two species. Although both may vary considerably in shade and markings, the grass snake is always a lustrous green, almost enamelled in appearance, while the adder is a dull, dirty brown.

There are other differences, less easily observed, all of them fascinating but none so useful for quick identification. The manner of their birth is very different. Grass snakes produce eggs; soft and beautiful like strings of pearls. They do not sit like birds to incubate them but lay them in warm places such as a manure heap, or carefully chosen sunny positions. Young adders on the other hand are born alive and are quickly able to fend for themselves.

Perhaps the most striking difference in habits is that the grass snake swallows its prey whole and alive. Frogs, toads or a great variety of smaller fry can be taken in without being bitten or chewed and can stay alive inside the snake for some time before being digested. The adder's method of killing and eating is the reason why we need to be able to identify it. It bites, has poisonous fangs and hollow teeth. At the root of each tooth is a bag of poison. When it bites, the poison enters the bloodstream of the victim and kills it. Fieldmice and shrews are easy targets, human beings are attacked in self defence, but the result can be just as conclusive.

The same afternoon that we watched the snake, a mother moorhen emerged from her nest, up towards the bridge, and paraded her jet black chicks before us. This was also a surprise as our old gander usually took steps to clear moorhens off what he regarded as his stretch of water. Perhaps on this occasion they agreed a truce and may even have spared a moment to admire each other's offspring, Harry being the proud and protective father of two tiny goslings.

A fortnight later, the moorhen's brood was reduced to two and our geese had lost both their young. Inevitably our thoughts went back to the snake but it is fairly certain that our old enemy, the rat, was responsible.

The building which we called our workshop and from which we enjoyed watching activities in the stream was a condemned one-up-one-down cottage with a lean-to kitchen at the back. It stood in our garden a few feet away from the cottage in which we lived. To use the building required planning permission for change of use and subsequent visits from the department for the purpose of re-valuation and re-rating.

We were only mildly surprised, after our earlier experiences in this field, to watch the little building being measured inside and out. Apparently no hidden accommodation was discovered within the thickness of its random flint walls or beneath its low slate roof. The floor was of yellow Suffolk brick. Two windows overlooked the brook. It was a delightful place in which to work and dream.

Being a romantic, I liked to think of that workshop as a living folk museum; a sort of shrine of craftsmanship compounded with a scented bower. It was a place in which I spent happy hours every day. There was even honeysuckle round the door.

There were indeed plenty of ingredients for an olfactory feast. Pure turpentine, beeswax, stoppers, fillers and sealers, paints and varnishes, ranged on the shelves. There was often some leather and saddlesoap about the place to vary the flavour.

The woodburning stove added its own pungency and sometimes, when I was doing a stint of rushwork, the sweet scent of dried rushes took over and held sway until the job was done.

It saddens and surprises me a little to recall that with so many delightful elements, the amalgam was not always a delight; the total result being somewhat less pleasant than any one of the ingredients.

As to antiquity, there were always some nice old pieces of furniture about and always a fair showing of old tools. Many of those which I used or kept in case I should ever have a use for them belonged to my wife's step-grandfather. He was by all accounts a kind and gentle man who more than tolerated a small girl who wanted to see how everything was done. He is happily remembered as are also some of his tools. Even now my wife will sometimes enquire, for example, where a certain broad-bladed chisel can be found. Which gives the cue for the apocryphal story of the man who said: "I'm using the same scythe my great-grandfather used. It's had four new snaithes and five new blades but that's the same one he used".

Usage and passage of time has made it necessary to replace some of the old tools and I have even been dragged kicking and screaming (as our son William would say) into the twentieth century, and have added some power handtools. The use of these never gives me much pleasure but I have to admit that they take some of the hard work out of certain

A rude Carpenter?

jobs.

Plastic handles on new chisels or screwdrivers are poor substitutes for proper turned wood with brass bands which give both visual and tactile pleasure. A steel handled hammer with synthetic rubber handgrip may well be a technological advance but it gives me no more 'spring' than a good ash handle which also provides a direct link right back to our early ancestors in these islands.

One of the times I liked best was when crisp wood-shavings lay in drifts around the feet of the bench and the air was filled with the sweet scent of pine forest as the blade of my plane bit into the dormant fragrance. At the other end of the scale was that abysmal business known as 'stripping'. It is a word which calls up various pictures for various people. For me it meant a nauseous session removing paint or varnish from pine furniture.

Yet even this vile process has its moments of reward. As the last of the gooey sludge is scraped and scrubbed away the beautiful grain and figuring of the good is revealed and the self-imposed penance all becomes worthwhile. Of course there are occasions when the removal of paint exposes untold horror in the form of filling or other chicanery which has been hidden from the eye. I was always glad to leave a stripping session and get back to the cosier atmosphere of the workshop.

It must be obvious that I am not a specialist. If pressed I enjoy describing myself as a rude carpenter. To tell the truth I turn my hand to a great variety of jobs, including upholstery, rush seating, metalwork and a wide range of virtually unclassifiable occupations which can only be lumped together under the heading of restoration.

We did not create in our workshop. We re-created. We cleaned, repaired and restored. We brought to light some of the craftsmanship of the past, much of which had been lost from sight behind layers of paint or just the grime and neglect of generations.

I have told of some of the scents and visual pleasure of the workshop, perhaps I should also mention sounds. I am not fond of music while I work but I am told that when I am happy I whistle endlessly and not always in tune. This must be very trying to others as I am excessively happy most of the time.

Beyond the workshop lay the barn. If you know East Anglia, then it probably sounds as if I am boasting when I say that this was the second barn which we had owned. You may well think of the vast and beautiful tithe barn at Paston, of its mellow brickwork and beautiful timbers, hammerbeams and Queenpost trusses which support the handsome and recently renewed Norfolk reed thatch. If North Norfolk is your stamping ground, then you may think of flint and pantile as seen for example at

Letheringsett and Binham. Almost anywhere in Norfolk and Suffolk you can see examples of tarred weather-boarding or even clay lump constructions. The variety and combinations of materials used seems to be endless.

I do not think that many can exceed the 163 feet length of the Paston barn but 100 feet or more is not uncommon. In line and beauty many such barns rival the local churches, often exceeding them in size and simple magnificence if not in decorative detail. If mention of a barn brings this sort of picture to your mind, then you are not thinking of our modest buildings.

The first of our barns adjoined our home in Norfolk, the plaque on the gable end proclaimed: 'ET 1940' but this end was clearly an addition; the original building was considerably older. From the pitch of its pantiled roof and the absence of signs of alterations, I do not think that it had ever been thatched. The soft red bricks of the walls were honeycombed with nooks and crevices much loved by wrens which made their homes within them. It was of such modest proportions that its width was barely sufficient to house the family car.

One end had been used as a stable, with signs of primitive living accommodation above and a simple form of pigeon loft in one gable end. We grew climbing roses and hydrangeas against the wall. It served us well in various capacities, even housing our caravan in winter. Finally, we stored all our furniture in it after we had sold the farmhouse and were living in the caravan while we looked for our next home which turned out to be the Old Forge.

The barn which we then owned was even smaller but had an uncertain charm and certainly did not lack antiquity. Part of the footings were made of random flint and brick; thin handmade bricks certainly of the style, if not in fact, of Roman origin. Though who will say with certainty that they were not? Here was a Roman road and local clay plentiful. The rest of the brickwork was of later date; a hard yellowish brick of indeterminate age, though certainly more recent than the three hundred year old cottage.

Soon after we went to live there, we started clearing the little barn and putting it in good order. The first step was to clear the surrounding growth of elderberry and brambles and to lop off the more instrusive branches of the oak tree. When we had done that we could see the size of the job. Our neighbour from up the hill looked in and said, "Good heavens! I'd forgotten that there was a building there". Even then it was snugly tucked in beneath an oak tree and almost hidden from the lane by a beech hedge. With its sound pantile roof and new weather-boarding at one side, it provided dry shelter and extra work space.

We dug out several inches of dried chicken droppings, in the expectation of finding a brick or cobble floor but seemingly there was never anything but beaten earth. The proportions of the doorway, and the positions of the pintles which had carried a two part stable door indicated that at one time a donkey was stalled there. We also discovered donkey shoes which added weight to the theory but did not necessarily prove it, being so close to the smithy.

One thing is sure and that is that while it has stood there, our barn had been used for a great variety of purposes including storage and the housing of livestock. Perhaps none more bizarre than the use to which we put it. The section at the far end became known as "the stripping room". Anything less erotic than scrubbing painted pine furniture with boiling caustic soda I find hard to imagine.

Our barn survived though it is clear that in spite of their multi-use potential a great many old barns have become outmoded by modern farming practice. Within half an hour's walk I can see a dozen fine specimens falling into decay, the cost of their maintenance exceeding their current usefulness.

Perhaps only the mighty tithe barns will be preserved, reminding us of twelve hundred years of turbulent history surrounding the gathering of "God's Portion" from the land.

I think that I have now set the scene and may move on to tell of some of our activities in the business which we created.

LOT 4
Have a nice Day

Looking back to the day when we opened our doors to the public, it is amazing to realise just how ill-prepared we were for all that was to happen. At least one leading bank issues a small book on the subject of "Starting your own business". The last paragraph reads as follows: "If after what you have read, you are still determined or even more convinced that you want to go it alone, come and talk to the manager of your nearest branch."

I think there is very little doubt that if we had read the booklet first, we would have been put right off the whole idea of starting our own business. The advice and warnings offered are all absolutely sound and worthy, and very daunting. I suppose that it would be too much to expect such an impeccable source even to hint that the exercise might be exceedingly funny and even pleasurable.

Customers, the booklet suggests, can be most tiresome people with awkward habits, strange ideas about credit and not necessarily have noticeably good manners. In this field, as in many others, our experiences have been much more pleasant than we ever thought possible. Not only pleasant but in many cases downright enjoyable, with a growing number of customers developing into good friends.

Our old forge, where we conducted our business, is a single storeyed building, so typical of its kind that I would say that its original purpose is instantly recognisable. The cottage alongside, in which we lived, is also thatched but of two storeys and eminently domestic in appearance. One customer revisited us after an interval of about six months. She walked straight into our living room in the cottage saying: "My word! You have made your shop look very different."

In fairness I should add that one other caller made a similar mistake. I answered the knock on the front door — few people around here use the front door so it was in any case a notable occasion. "Good afternoon," said the stranger, "may I look around?"

"Certainly," I replied, and it didn't take long to establish that he too had come to the wrong building.

If we try to stand back and impersonally classify our customers (in the manner recommended by the bank booklet when making our survey of the potential market), the first two clear categories are "trade" and "private". As a sweeping generalisation, it could be said that a private customer will take 90 minutes to spend five pounds, while a trade buyer will spend ninety pounds in five minutes. It was certainly yet another surprise, at least to us innocents, that well over 80 per cent of our business was conducted with trade buyers.

We feel that more by luck than any judgement we got this balance just about right. To become all "trade" would, we believe, make the business much less personal. We could come to regard our stock as mere merchandise, and then we might just as well as buying and selling bags of salt. Involvement with our stock-in-trade and our customers made our way of life a happy and endlessly changing prospect.

Quite often it happened that we had a by-gone which baffled us — was it for taking the eyes out of potatoes? Or perhaps countersinking screws? Before lone someone would come along and tell us. They might buy it first and then tell us that for fifty pence they had become the proud owner of a rare silversmith's tool known as a "scrimer".

If we kept quiet and listened, a whole range of expert knowledge and opinion was paraded before us and also a fair leavening of misinformation. One of my favourite eavesdropping situations was listening to a know-it-all husband handing out erroneous information to an all-trusting spouse. I never offered an opinion or information unless invited to do so. We heard some ingenious dissertations on the use of such things as wooden poster type, goffering irons, drawknives and timberdogs.

We got on well with our overseas customers, some from as far away as Tasmania. We enjoyed inscrutable Danes, punctilious Germans, charming Netherlanders and one hilarious Belgian with whom we communicated in execrable French. He came over on the ferry and usually made us his first call, so out came the coffee pot and we got straight into our "French without tears" act.

Americans, too, both temporary residents from USAAF bases and buyers from the States who came over at fairly regular intervals, all added to the cheerful activities which suddenly revitalised the old forge. The smithy as a meeting place for exchange of gossip and news had again taken on one of its traditional roles.

Our first year in the business passed so quickly that I was amazed to find that it was time for stocktaking and getting the books up-to-date ready for our Accountant. I am happy to record that we had found an Accountant with a great sense of humour — another welcome novelty.

I suppose that my first encounter with the tedious business of a complete physical check and total accountability was Saturday morning kit inspection. "One on, one at the laundry, and one laid out for inspection, sir!" might have explained away the absence of a missing shirt K.D. It was no alibi for items such as a Spanner Macmahorn 14 inch, whatever that was, or two tables barrackroom 6 ft, which had inadevertently been used in the process of extracting a three-ton lorry from a ditch.

As my interests and involvements have changed, so too, has the character of the annual stocktake. Sacks of soap powder, gallons of cleaning fluid and all the many items used in the laundry and cleaning trade right down to pens and pencils, gave way to reams and reams of paper and many pounds of printer's ink.

I am sure that few people other than printers have any idea of the multiplicity of different papers which are made. The range of colour is that of the rainbow; substance, texture and finish, and then the range of sizes can make life very confusing at all times, not least at stocktaking. There are special purpose papers, too, such as self-adhensives and fluorescent and at the end of the line there are papers which aren't really paper at all, but plastic.

I don't remember much trouble with ink. At least all the tins carried labels and if the writing was illegible it was only because of a surfeit of spillage which clearly identified itself.

By and large, those stocktakings were a bore; trying aftermaths to the New Year's celebrations, with really nothing to commend them, not even the relative ease with which they could be carried out.

It might not immediately have struck you on entering our old forge that here was a business which could be involved in such a mundane matter as stocktaking. I am told that the atmosphere was a mixture of a forge, a farmhouse kitchen and a folk museum. Certainly our stock in trade include a wide range of items useful curious and beautiful; it is this which made the annual roll-call a diversion rather than a labour.

That first time we started on the job, we hadn't got far before we came to an oak bureau. It was what you might call a "sticker" which had been with us rather too long. What made this the more surprising is that desks and bureaux can usually be relied on to move quickly. We tried to look at it dispassionately. What was wrong with it? The price seemed reasonable — we couldn't sensibly reduce that enough to make any difference. Its condition was fair and, even if it couldn't be described as a handsome piece, it was serviceable and in good working order. One handle was loose and as I had been meaning to attend to it, now seemed like a good moment. then we gave it a good polish all over. Perhaps if it was moved to a new position it would catch the eye better.

Just moving a bureau to a new position sounds like the work of a few minutes but if you recall the old expression used by the tightly packed family, 'When father turns, we all turn'', then you will quickly realise that in order to move one piece of furniture it is often necessary to move eight or nine other pieces and that is precisely what we had to do.

In the middle of that upheaval, some customers came in. Then it was time for a cup of coffee. Two telephone calls and one more customer later we were back at the oak bureau with the stock-book and checked off happily till lunchtime.

After lunch we started on chairs. Now, I enjoy chairs; not so much fine Chippendale or Hepplewhite styles, and certainly not most upholstered varieties, but good honest country chairs in all their wealth of styles and variations from the seventeenth to early twentieth century.

You could say with much truth that my taste is not sophisticated, but I will still hotly defend a Boston rocker or a low-backed Windsor of Mendlesham type as designs not since surpassed or even equalled.

I can easily go off at a tangent when I get among the chairs, polishing the wonderful grain of elm seats, admiring the rushwork seats of ladderbacks and the endless variations on a theme to be found in the turned legs and spindles.

By teatime we were back among the hand tools, checking off awls, augers and adze, bettle, billhooks and butterparts through to mauls, mattock and waggon-jack. I recognised a dealer's car turning into the lane and put the stockbook aside for a spell. This dealer travelled a route through East Anglia so we could look forward to news of friends and acquaintances and, with reasonable luck, to transacting some business.

But the time some of our stock had disappeared into his capacious Volvo we were ready to call it a day; a day of pleasurable activity and of profit. Stocktaking could wait till tomorrow.

The blacksmith's bellows in one corner of our old forge were not for sale. The last smith who worked there died only recently but the bellows remained unused for over 30 years. They stood more than six feet tall; two huge slabs of elm darkened by age and use to the same stygian hues as the leather which joined them and the close rows of metal studs along their edges.

The almost surgical contrivance of leather which swathed the joint with its metal spout reminded me somewhat of Long John Silver and his wooden leg. This thought apart, they were a satisfying object to have around. Their massive strength proclaimed a fitness of purpose symbolic of all the best qualities which we associate with that almost mythical character, the Village Blacksmith.

In spite of our resolution not to sell our one remaining link with the former activities in the old forge, we were able to fulfil a number of requests to supply old blacksmith's bellows. You might ask who would want to buy such things. I can only relate our own experiences.

One such customer was a French ex-schoolmistress. It was not immediately obvious to us why she bought a large set of bellows. In fact we wondered about her for some weeks. We were delighted when she came back to the forge and told us her story.

She had removed the passenger seat from her Mini and with considerable skill and some help had managed to stow the bellows in its place, entirely filling that side of the car. Then she set off for a holiday in France. She more than half expected problems with Customs, but no, it was smiles and salutes all the way. "Mais oui, of course Madame would take un souffle with her on holiday. Bon voyage!"

Comfortably on her way to the shores of the Mediterranean, Madame had sold the bellows. She sold them so well that her object in coming to see us again was not to tell us the story but to place a repeat order in anticipation of her next year's holiday.

The Belgian who bought a similar set was undeniably a dealer. He said he was buying them for a museum of rural life. At least I think that is what he said. As we communicated only in execrable French I may have misunderstood him.

If, like another of our customers, your job is interior design for a firm of brewers, then you can be expected to be in the market for specialised or unusual items. The first set of bellows which this man bought from us was not the conventional shape. They were of the vertical cylindrical type which seem to have come on the market at about the time of the Great Exhibition. I believe that they would have taken over entirely had they not themselves been superseded by even more sophisticated equipment such as centrifugal fans and power driven mechanical blowers.

When the lever was worked up and down, the lower half of the "concertina" worked as a pump while the upper half, filled with the pressure of air, rose to form a reservoir. When a state of balance was achieved, air was delivered from the outlet in a fairly steady stream instead of a succession of blasts.

The whole assembly complete with its counterweights weighed over 250 pounds so it had been quite a performance getting it home from the saleground. During the time it spent on our forecourt it proved to be an eye-catcher. Few people could resist holding the cow horn handle at the end of the lever and pumping a few strokes — not unlike pulling up a point of beer in the good old manner.

The largest set of bellows which we handled was also the least blackened and were in remarkably good condition. We were able to clean the leatherwork with saddlesoap and restore its suppleness. The straight-grained slabs of elm which formed its sides turned to a rich honey colour as the dry wood soaked up wax and became a good polished surface.

It was indeed a thing of great beauty. We placed it on a pair of beer crates and arranged on it some hand-thrown pottery. We were not surprised when it stayed with us only a short time before being shipped out to Texas as a coffee table.

Some people might be horrified and deplore such "misuse" of an object. I like to think that we saved it from dereliction and decay, that we found a new home for it where it will continue to be appreciated and to give pleasure as an evocative reminder of other days and different standards.

My first close encounter with the US Military involved a Pilot and a Sergeant. Between them they managed to despatch me from a mean one thousand feet into the wrong part of Africa. From that poor beginning, more than forty years ago, relationships could only improve and I am happy to say that they have done so.

Our most colourful memories of cultural exchanges are of the times when we were invited to set up our stall at the Bazaar run by the US Officers' Wives Club.

The Bazaar has become an annual event, from the proceeds of which they finance a number of projects including two scholarships and three major contributions to charities. The vast No. 7 Hangar comfortably accommodates over one hundred and fifty traders, all there by invitation, with stands offering a wide range of goods. It would be hard to pick the least expected item among a galaxy which ranges from beautiful rocking horses, studio pottery right through to waterbeds, antiques and bygones.

On our first appearance, we arrived in good time to present ourselves with all the documentation, proofs of identity and special passes with which we had been provided. The guard on the gate was armed but showed very little interest in us beyond a genial wave and a flashing smile.

We proceeded at the regulation speed, following signs to the hangar. It is, I suppose, one of the biggest buildings into which I have been, making Norwich Cathedral seem like a parish church or the old Boulton

& Paul hangars on Mousehold like corrugated iron garages.

By the time we had set up our display, the feverish cold which had been creeping up on me all day was really making itself felt. We drove away from the bright lights of the hangar into the dark concrete labyrinth of the base. Somewhere I missed the exit route and a growing feeling of hallucination was increased when we found ourselves driving between rows of sinister F One Elevens. I knew we were wrong.

Our caravan park was not far enough away. My fevered brain was tortured by jet engines sucking in the night air, consuming it with devastating roars and cutting out with such abruptness as to leave withdrawal symptoms. Dawn came slowly.

At ten o'clock on Saturday morning, doors were officially opened. My feelings of unreality were greatly increased as the crowd built up. All the 'extras' and bit-part players you have ever seen from 'Gone with the Wind' thru 'M.A.S.H.' and 'Oklahoma' seemed to be there in their hundreds and some of the stars. I felt sure that J.R. was around but couldn't see him. Baseball caps jostled with stetsons, cryptic tee-shirts with their mysterious messages thronged with strange uniforms and elaborately decorated windcheaters. And with them, their wives and children.

American women take charm seriously and work at it to good effect. It rubs off on their children, too. One trait which I greatly admire is their ability to accept a compliment gracefully. If, for example, one admires a dress, the response is always on the lines of, "Thank you very much, I'm glad you like it", rather than, "What, this old thing? I've had it for ages!"

There was an occasion when I delivered a pine settle a little ahead of schedule. The colonel's lady was taking a shower. She came to the door in her bathrobe, leaving a trial of wet footprints down the hallway.

"I've gotta go to this coffee morning", she explained, "and I have to make myself beautiful."

"You'll have no difficulty with that", said I in my most gallant Southern manner.

"Oh, thank you", she said, and then left me wondering by adding, "I guess you're not typical."

In the bright lights of the hangar, colour, movement and noise all built up into a great air of festivity. Quite soon the scent of barbecured spare ribs wafted in from the tarmac outside. For two days we ate on such delicacies as these, spring rolls, popcorn and burgers with an endless supply of coffee supplied by our hostesses.

There was plenty of brisk business being conducted as well, and we were happy to have a part in this. You may have noted that I am well

44

on the way towards being bi-lingual, but I confess that with an exchange rate of 1.72, I was not very speedy on sterling/dollar conversions. The fact that we were dealing in both currencies underlined the strangeness of the situation. This was clearly a little piece of America transported to East Anglia. Just for the moment, roles were reversed and we were the visitors, our friends the hosts. For friends they are: good friends and peacekeeping allies — facts which no political bickering or lunatic fringe demonstrations can tarnish.

On Friday nights when I was a child my father used to shut the front garden gate. Early next morning there would be drovers herding cattle along Newmarket Road to the slopes below the castle. When the cattle market was moved to Harford bridges it meant that we no longer had need to shut our gate, but it meant far more than that for it changed the character of the city and was the first of many major sacrifices on the altar of the automotive god.

Happily such drastic change has not taken place in all our market towns. Some cattle markets have closed and disappeared but there are still weekly produce markets with their ancient origins and royal charters and their weekly gatherings in sale yards and auction rooms.

The scene, once found, has always the same basic ingredients. The goods offered tend to have a certain sameness, but the passing pageant of humanity never fails to intrigue me. If there is a common denominator among these fascinating collections of people it is not easily seen.

Not all of us are seeking bargains, some have bought goods to sell, many I am sure come for the social occasion which it offers. Even among the bargain seekers there are the curious, the opportunists, the collectors and of course the dealers. Some will tell you that dealers are a breed apart but this is a misappellation for to be of a breed implies at least distinguishing characteristics if not actual common ancestry. In truth dealers are at least as diverse as any other group of people who happen to have a common interest.

Attending sales is on balance a tedious occupation, not unlike panning for gold. A few small grains from time to time keep one going, always living in hope or expectation of finding a sizeable nugget; of spotting the swan which everyone else believes to be a goose.

One of the great virtues of this necessity was that it took me to a number of market towns in East Anglia, always visiting them on the liveliest day of the week, as market day in the country remains the focal point of the working week. The sleepiest of market places wakes up and the human race parades in all its interesting diversity.

At Sudbury, down on the Suffolk border, the weekly stock sale and the auction of miscellaneous goods are almost inextricably mixed. In that sale yard, I saw an artist at work and stepped back to view the scene from where he stood. He had captured that small moment of drama and do-it-yourself choreography which is repeated endlessly around the sale yards; the grouping and regrouping as the centre of interest shifts with successive lots. He had captured the attitudes of concentration so noticeable at Sudbury where it is often impossible to hear the auctioneer until the last of the pigs have been sold and loaded noisily into transporters.

I find the sale room at North Walsham to be one of the most civilized. There is no need to watch what one might be treading in, nor is there a feeling that the cattle will be allowed back in as soon as the final lot has been sold. Aylsham is the hottest or the coldest depending on the time of the year. It always rains at Stalham, which is why I was bidding for a bundle of walking sticks and umbrellas the last time I was there. It was above average luck that for two pounds fifty one of the umbrellas kept me reasonably dry, one of the horn handled sticks had a solid silver band and the other was gold plated!

I could catalogue thus the salerooms of Norfolk and Suffolk and parallel each with a description of the auctioneer, for if dealers are a gallimaufry of individuals, auctioneers are no less so. The ones who win my admiration are those who, without bullying, manage to maintain a reasonable degree of quietness among the crowd, who get through their work expeditiously and who enliven the proceedings from time to time with a few shafts of wit.

"Lot 4. One stuffed dog in glass case. Turn it round, Fred, so I can't see it. Now who will say five pounds? Four? Three? Who will give it a good home for a pound?"

A little humour helps for there is often an element of sadness at these sales. Many pathetic items are offered; small things which clearly meant much to their owners but now are scorned at fifty pence and put with the next lot — "One carpet. What state is it in, Fred?" "Been walked on." Fred and his fellows can make or mar a sale; they are good men to have as friends.

There is one other character of note at every sale. He is the 'runner' who shuffles in and out of the scene at regular intervals but has no lines to speak. He conveys the sales sheets to the office, a little haven set somewhat apart from the hurly-burly where with amazing speed and dexterity detailed bills are prepared for settlement before we collect our newly acquired chattels. We pack them then into our estate cars and lash

46

them on our roof racks. The pigs and cattle are also departing in trucks; we are all driving or driven but there is not a drover in sight.

During our days at the Old Forge my wife became our chief buyer. William and I looked after the shop and, when we weren't watching wildlife in the stream, worked at cleaning and restoring the trophies brought home to us.

Our chief buyer quickly became astute and very successful. Occasionally we had to cry for mercy and plead for some respite in which to catch up with a backlog of work. When long distances were involved I was allowed to attend sales and on some memorable occasions William and I had a day out together.

If you want an entertaining day out, I can recommend going with William in a hired van to collect a load of furniture. Mind you, you will earn your keep all right but there will be some good laughs along the way.

I should say that in the field of employment, I have led a more sheltered, less adventurous life than he. He did, for example, during his self-sufficiency period, work part-time for a small but energetic furniture removal firm, so that he has professional experience in this field.

On our first time time out together on a collecting job, I was amazed to find him so entirely in command of the situation. Completely at home up there behind the wheel in the cab, suddenly he was the ''Yorkie Man'', smiling and courteous to other road-users, eating up the mileage and wearing competence like a well laundered boilersuit.

But for the fact that we had studied the map together the evening before, I would have sworn that he knew the route like the back of his hand, right down to picking the best cafe for value and knowing where petrol was twopence a gallon cheaper.

This first job we did together was not exactly a house clearance, it was a stable clearance! Not Augean, but a very civilised affair down in Berkshire. The stable block in question was due for conversion to a cottage for the daughter of the owners. Happily it had not housed horses for many years but had been used for generations as the junk room.

Nor had it been a straightforward task to make an estimate and give a quotation for the job. Until we were well advanced with the clearance it had been quite impossible to see what was actually there, let alone assess the condition of the various items.

One of the unexpected things among the murk was a serpentine fronted Italian commode. Although it was nearly seven feet long, we had not even seen it until we had removed much of the lumber. Back at the Old Forge, it took us two and half days just to remove the accumulation of chicken droppings and clean that one piece of furniture.

Only then could we begin to appreciate its magnificence and value. We sold it well and although with hindsight we may have 'given it away', it made everyone happy and justified the whole operation.

On another clearance job, we were invited and could hardly refuse, to deliver a bureau to an address in London not far off our route homeward. We found the place without trouble and discovered the flat was up three flights of stairs.

"Now," said William, "when you are offered a tip, no silly nonsense about it, just accept it gracefully."

We groaned and grunted up the stairs. Madam showed us where to lower our burden. No, perhaps that wasn't the best place, please move it over here. What did Charles think? Wasn't that better? or perhaps after all she ought to have it over there where the light would come over her left shoulder. Yes, that was definitely the right place so it could now be moved forward and be dusted before being lifted against the wall.

With somewhat distant thanks, we were dismissed. There was certainly no tip to be received gracefully; not even the offer of a cup of tea. We went back down to the van and laughed all the way to Hyde Park Corner, especially when we thought of the two electricity outlets which the bureau had masked in it final resting place.

To be able to judge how much can be stowed in a van and the best way to do it is something which comes with experience. In the same way, three dimensional thinking becomes second nature after many experiences of trying to fit furniture into other people's cars. Almost invariably, the owners of expensive cars think that it follows naturally that it must have a large capacity. "Oh, yes!" they say airily, "I've got an NBG Six, we can easily put that little chest in the boot" and you know full well you've got another delivery job imminent.

On the other hand, houses and furniture have evolved more or less together so that it is normally possible to get furniture in or out without too much difficulty. There are exceptions which even defeat William and such stratagems as taking out window frames or going over the next door neighbour's wall and in through the back door.

A specially large pine refectory table nearly defeated us on one occasion. We failed to introduce it into the kitchen/living room by any normal means. "There's only one thing to do," said our customer, "and that is to knock off that bar so that you can get the legs round the door post."

"Yes," replied William, "I can see that, but there is just one other point. Whose table is it?"

"Point taken," agreed the customer, who wrote out a cheque and produced a large hammer.

There is one ridiculous postscript to these notes. When my wife and I moved into our cottage, none of our furniture could be got up the stairs or through the little windows under the thatch. Even William was defeated.

Of course one tends to forget the defeats, the mistakes and minor disasters and to remember the small trimphs — Lot 99 was one of these.

It stood in the old cattle pens outside the sale-room. It was the only item in the weekly sale in which I was seriously interested. There was quite a pretty tin hip-bath, though its decorative paintwork was past salvation; an elm drop-leaf table much frequented by wood beetles and a dough bin in similar condition.

With practised nonchalance and probably fooling no-one but myself, I examined it carefully, overtly making a more enthusiastic appraisal of Lot 100, a bedroom suite of truly horrific appearance.

In my 1880 edition of Mrs Beeton's Household Management there is a page of illustrations showing some of the larger and essential pieces of equipment for a Victorian kitchen. Among them is what Mrs Beeton describes as a ''meat screen'' and notes that it cost 3 guineas. It is also known as a proving-cupboard so it is clearly a case of an adaptable piece of equipment which you can call whatever you fancy and use to your own best advantage.

So there in the cattle pen stood Lot 99, a filthy disgrace to any kitchen but with the pure lines of a veteran and, beauty being in the eye of the beholder, a highly desirable example of genuine antique kitchenalia.

In essentials, a proving cupboard is a portable cupboard with no back, usually of pine lined with tin sheet. It is furnished with two or three shelves and a carrying handle on each of its curved ends. When used for its intended purposes, it was placed in front of a fire. Plates, dishes, tureens could be warmed or kept warm with their contents. If used for proving, the kneaded dough was placed on its shelves to rise preparatory to baking. When not in use it could be lifted aside from the fire. Today these relics are often found to have had backs added, to have been painted and with metal liners removed.

There was a fair crowd at the sale. Most of the usual faces and all those truly amazing people one seems to find only at auction sales. it is one of my unfulfilled dreams to become a quick-fire artist, able to produce lightning sketches of people's faces. I have, as Henry James understood it, been granted my subject but have been able to make nothing of it.

Vigorous ringing of a hand-bell brought me back to earth. The auctioneer joked his way through his brief preliminary remarks and offered Lot 1, a child's desk which he assured us would make any child's preparation for 'O' Levels a real pleasure. And so on, through the cattle pens and the heterogeneous collection of surplus, discarded and surely unloved furniture and effects.

"Lot 42. Now here's a beauty! What shall we say for this dressing table? Who will start me at £20? £10? Come on now, somebody help me with an offer. All right then, it's firewood" and with appreciative laughter, he extracted an offer of 50 pence and passed to Lot 43, a sad collection of five odd chairs.

As often seems to happen, prices were low that day except in the case of the few items for which I could raise even mild enthusiasm. The half dozen lots preceding the cupboard were carpets. The crowd and interest thinned noticeably, then quite suddenly it quickened again and I knew that I had some competition.

The choreography of a sale-ground crowd is almost as fascinating as the faces. It surges, swells and diminishes in everchanging density, arranging and re-arranging itself around the principal performers, the auctioneer and his clerk, as they move from item to item.

Even now I feel the drama of these little occasions. I am conscious of a quickening pulse as I enter a contest and start putting in my bids. Experience has taught me that I must not let emotion cloud my judgement. It is my almost invariable rule to decide on my limit long before the bidding starts.

"Lot 99, ladies and gentlemen; a useful cupboard. I have an advance bid of £50 and can take any improvement on that."

Fifty five, thank you. Sixty, sixty five, seventy to the gentleman on my left. Anyone else? Sold!"

All over in about thirty seconds and the "useful cupboard" was mine.

The filth in which it was encrusted was largely superficial. I never doubted that back in our workshop, the pine would again glow and respond to wax polishing. There are great satisfactions to be found in works of restoration. There is hard-earned profit, too. the speed with which this particular item was sold in our forge was quite breathtaking.

Another triumph which my wife likes to recall, and she had many to her credit, was a well-sinker's windlass. She bought it at a sale of builders materials and had to telephone for William to help get it back to the forge. This unusual object so stirred my imagination that I took some trouble to find out more about its use and history.

My search for englightenment led me to a village in the Stour Valley. To use the word provenance in connection with such a piece of equipment may seem pretentious and over pedantic, but like many other bygones and relics from the past which come into our hands, the well-sinker's windlass had demanded investigation.

The stout wooden roller, iron-bound at its ends, had an obvious fitness of purpose. At each end, winding handles, in common with all other metal parts, were blacksmith-made, each piece with its own touch of individuality and restrained ornamentation. This applied most specially to the butterfly nuts used in bolting together the wooden beams which supported the roller. Even these beams had been planed, chamfered and painted. the horizontal tie-bar carried part of a sign-written legend:

"A. SPINK, Plumber etc ... Church Street ..."

It didn't take me too long to track down the grandson of A. Spink. Even though he was not able to give me a first-hand account of well-sinking, my prompting stirred memories of his early days when grandfather was active.

"No, I never went down, nor didn't father. Grandfather was the last well-sinker in this family. They don't sink wells like that no more but I know all about it. My family have been here near on a hundred and fifty years. You'll see our names up there in the church."

"We've all been builders. there isn't nothing in the building trade we don't know and that includes funerals and sinking wells if it come to it."

"Proper bricked up wells I'm speaking of, not deep-bore and pipes nor even concrete cylinder jobs."

"First thing was to clear the site and get all the gear and materials together. He never knew for sure how long a sweat it was going to be nor how many bricks he would need."

"When he'd decided on the position, he marked out a circle, say five or six feet across and removed the turf. Then the digging started. Two men at a time. It was easy to start with and got more difficult from then on. Not much room in the circle for two men. After they were down about five feet they used short-handled spades. Even then if they didn't work well together they could fetch each other some nasty clouts."

"Grandfather knew all about soil. If it was crumbly and unsafe they started bricking up sooner than if it was firm. It was important to check the sides of the hole with a vertical plumb line. If they didn't start straight, they never would get it right. He was a-checking with his plumb from then on. I shouldn't wonder if that wasn't how we come to be called plumbers."

When grandfather decided that it was time to start bricking up, he had the floor of the hole cleared and levelled. They set four quarter-plates in the bottom. Good, solid oak or elm quadrants which were bolted together to form a circle. The first course of bricks was laid on the circle and built up course by course until they reached the top of the hole. They then laid a second set of wooden quadrants on top of the bricks. This wooden ring was then connected to the bottom one with chains tightened

51

with bottle-screws to hold all the brickwork rigid.

Now was the time to rig the windlass over the hole. A strong rope was wound on the roller and an oversize 'dog clip' spliced into the free end. A large bucket or special wooden platform could be clipped on. From now on the wind-lass was in almost constant use. With a pair of hands on each of the two handles, men and materials were lowered and spoil from the digging raised for disposal on the surface.

As digging went on, the weight of the brickwork on the lower quadrants was supported by carefully placed struts and footblocks. The most hazardous moments occurred every time the digging had gone deep enough for the careful removal of these supports. With a creaking, slithering, muted rumble, the whole cylindrical construction slid down to the new bottom.

When that shuddering moment was safely past and the dirt had settled, the diggers were hauled to the surface for a well-earned breather. The top quadrants were removed and once again bricks laid up to the top of the hole, quadrants replaced and chains tightened. This routine was repeated time and again, day after day, until water in sufficient quantity was found.

"It wasn't everyone who liked working forty or fifty feet down," said Mr Spink, "and it was hard work on the handles of that windlass what you bought. But then, nobody hasn't turned them handles for more than forty years."

Wellsinkers Windlass.

LOT 5
A Funny Business

Farm disposal sales usually have a strong element of sadness, especially when the catalogue ends up with 'miscellaneous equipment and household effects'. It is often a pathetic sight to see the worn tools and relics of a working life laid out on the grass for all to see.

This one was rather different. We happened to know the farmer-cum-publican who was giving up the farming side of his activities in order to concentrate on the catering. The situation was one which reminded us of a recent holiday among the Greek Islands, where it is becoming a common sadness to see vineyards, olive and citrus groves left untended by their owners who find it more lucrative to engage in one or another aspect of tourism.

In this case, the piggeries were to be demolished to make room for holiday chalets, the stockyard would become a car park and sundry outbuildings were scheduled for demolition and replacement by an extension to the pub.

There were, in all, 550 Lots assembled for sale by auction on Saturday at 10.00 a.m. sharp. They ranged from 1 Bull Calf, 3 St Kilda Ewes and some Goats, to one dog kennel, muck fork and bucket, by way of a Range Rover, Wacker Werke hardcore compressor and 50 bales of hay.

We were lucky enough to be given a personally conducted preview the evening before the sale. I say lucky enough, because so often one looks at items offered for sale and trots out the well-worn phrase, "if only it could speak and tell its story". In this case, our friend was the third generation to have filled the dual post of landlord and farmer so was able to enlighten us.

"Take that old pig-bench, for example. They wouldn't want to have that if they'd seen as many pigs laid out on it and butchered as I have." it was also beyond his comprehension that anyone could wish to hang old rat-traps on a wall for decoration. "Wicked things they were — very effective, but sometimes the jaws snapped together so sharp they'd cut a rat's leg off."

"Now, that old Windsor chair you've got your eye on, that belonged to my father and his before then. My father used to sit in it over there by the back porch. A nice warm corner in the afternoon sunshine. When he couldn't do much else, mother used to give the old chap a basket of peas to shell or some other job from the kitchen just so that he didn't feel he was useless.''

''I don't know how that chair come to lose one arm, it's been up in the shed ever since father died.''

''So have those walking sticks. The ash one he bought for himself when he took me to some sheepdog trials in Wales. The silver topped one was a Silver Wedding present. I think you are right, I didn't ought to sell that — I'll slip it out now before it's too late. The Malacca cane probably belonged to my uncle Peter, he was the sailor in the family.''

''You know about those milking stools and the carrying yoke, but you might not recognise all those odd tools. My other uncle, Stephen, was a thatcher. We didn't have all his tools though most of them are here. He made them himself with a little help from the blacksmith in the village.''

''Those bottle-jacks have been in the corner of the cart shed as long as I can remember. They haven't been used for forty years, not since the last tumbril went. Blossom went at the same time. Those are some of her old shoes among the other scrap-iron, and that harness was hers, too.''

The day of the sale was bright and sunny. A pretty day, as our American friends are apt to express it. The whole scene was like market day in miniature. Cars soon choked the narrow roads and were parked in all directions. The pub opened its doors at nine and the whole family pitched in to a fourteen hour stint of profitable activity. Perhaps it is because of my upbringing, or just the habit of a lifetime, that the thought of beer at 9.00 a.m. is quite repugnant. But it is only a matter of degree, as ten thirty is entirely acceptable, or even ten o'clock at a pinch.

With much ringing of a hand bell and the usual preamble by the auctioneer, selling started promptly as advertised. Livestock and deadstock were sold simultaneously, the junior auctioneer being delegated to dispose of the 'miscellaneous effects'. He was a competent young man who got on with his job without waste of time, injecting just sufficient wit to keep the crowd in cheerful mood.

My wife, as I have indicated, is an experienced buyer. Shrewd and efficient, she had one fault. If she had bought a really horrific mixed lot of domestic jetsam for the sake of one item, such as a carved breadboard, she was incapable of taking the trophy and leaving the rubbish behind. We got lumbered with such embarrassments as fourteen damaged plastic buckets, a rusty tin trunk full of chipped china, a cardboard box full of cutlery or five dubious oil stoves.

Nevertheless one of the many attractive aspects of dealing in antiques and bygones is that acquiring stock can never consist of writing out dull routine orders to wholesale suppliers. From the start it becomes a matter of personal involvement and judgement and of visits to a great variety of possible sources. The nearest we ever came to what might be called routine was a programme of attendances at auction sales.

These engagements formed a fairly regular pattern of dates in our diary but were far from routine in content. They are in fact rather like visits to a theatre with a resident repertory company. The principal participants are the same but the 'props' are different every week, and there is always an interchange of social chit-chat which makes up for a certain sameness in the script. Some auctioneers are better than average at a little ad lib and an occasional topical joke.

Many of the articles which we bought and sold evoked nostalgic memories of childhood or conjured up evocative pictures of an even more distant past. There were, for example, a pair of oxen shoes which stayed with us only a short time before being pounced on with joy by a collector of agricultural bygones. They were no more than two slithers of iron shaped rather like a pair of quotation marks. They spoke of a form of husbandry that survived in this country from Roman times until the early years of the twentieth century; an age now departed from Western civilisation though still lingering in some parts of the world.

We can still see horses being shod and it is notable that the horse is usually a willing or at least acquiescent party to the event. The bovine intellect on the other hand does not run to lifting up its feet as a horse can be trained to do. They were therefore thrown on their backs on the soft turf, their feet tied in a bunch while the blacksmith nailed on the eight shoes. An ox-boy sat enthroned on the great creature's neck to restrain its struggles.

An altogether rural and idyllic picture, so different from that evoked by, perhaps, a ''Blackhead Remover'' patented in 1908, or that seven-feet long pine and elm pig-bench on which a slaughtered pig would have been carried and dismembered but which, after many hours work, is reborn as a solid and distinguished coffee table.

My wife and I were often surprised by the comments of the young about items which were so familiar to us in childhood that we saw little odd about them and were indeed somewhat pained to realise that they can now be regarded as quaint, collectable relics from the past. We never thought that everyday household articles such as flat irons, stone hot water bottles or even range plates and coalhole covers would be sought after, but one can only agree that these and many other things have gained a beauty of solid merit alongside their gimmickly plastic and chrome successors.

The list of strange and interesting objects passing through our hands seemed endless. Our opening stock included a Panama straw hat, a four feet by six feet oil painting of a junk yard and a badly broken oriental vase, all abandoned by the previous owner of the property. Since then we lost count, but estimate that in seven years we handled at least seven thousand articles. They varied in size from six-foot high pine wardrobes, seven-feet wide Italian commodes and huge pine farmhouse tables to cobblers lasts, horseshoes, trinkets, medals and hat pins.

Although value is by no means always directly related to size or the physical effort involved, the range of prices was just as great; from ten pence to over a thousand pounds.

The degree of usefulness was also on a sliding scale. Twenty-four wooden milliners blocks of 1930 vintage were certainly interesting, even beautiful, but we would not have been surprised if they had stayed 'on the shelf' for rather longer than a couple of weeks. We could see that the nave from the centre of a huge waggon wheel had an uncertain charm but we were foolishly doubtful about its ready saleability. A friend had asked ''Who on earthy will buy a thing like that?'' The answer was her husband.

There were of course 'bread and butter'' lines such as stripped pine chests of drawers and almost any good quality stripped pine, sets of chairs and farmhouse kitchen tables. For the rest, there seemed to be no rule for success. The only guideline was that if we have been foolish enough to buy some strange, beautiful and probably useless article, then there was quite certain to be someone else a percentage more foolish than us.

Some of the more extravagantly useless bygones which have passed through our hands we rationalised as being 'conversation pieces'. I can recall a fair number of such items, ranging in size from that knave of a waggon wheel to the well-sinker's windlass. A great many objects in between certainly had some claim to beauty and also utility. Many could be used by flower arrangers. I hardly need add that these latter included vessels from dairy, stable, chemists shops, obscure corners of industry and, of course, from kitchens, hospitals and bed chambers.

It is, I feel, a natural and entirely harmless foible to decorate our homes or to seek to decorate a conversation. I am much taken with the thought that conversation may need preparation, rehearsal even or the predispositioning of stimulating objects. Salting the mine, as it were, and laying one's plans. How can I best guide the conversation gently towards bio chemistry? Have I got the punchline right for that story about my mother-in-law in the paternoster? Shall I put the stuffed parrot on the mantelpiece or on top of the corner cupboard.

Now I come to think of it, this sort of action is really only an adult extension of something we did when young. We loved to frequent a little joke shop in High Holborn where we bought such items as whoopee cushions, imitation flies on lumps of sugar, plastic fried eggs and "Naughty Fido". Practical jokes, yes, but great stimulants to animated conversation. I note that the Oxford Concise defines a conversation piece as a painting of a group of people, especially members of a family, arranged as if in conversation. Usage seems to be taking the phrase into wider fields.

That good conversation is an art I have never doubted, any more than I realise that its gift is unevenly distributed. Most of us have only to think of our own family group. Their abilities in this sphere range from scintillating to downright boring.

Am I being unjust or are you still with me? Have you got an uncle who never actually converses but who is exceedingly good at getting his back to the fire and delivering a monologue? Or an aunt who made up her mind about everything a great many years ago and sees no reason to reconsider matters? On the other end of the scale, you probably have an aunt or an uncle or even a parent who not only has a great fund of conversation and stories based on experience, but is also genuinely interested in your views and activities.

The Rev. Francis Kilvert notes in his diary" .. sat opposite Louisa Wyatt who talked Switzerland and saved me much trouble finding conversation.'' Dinner parties tend to be less formal than in his time but we all know a 'Louisa Wyatt' who is liable to produce an over large pile of photographs or, even worse, sits us down to a display of colour slides of those boring old bears in Berne.

It is always pleasant to be able to introduce an interesting subject, to drop a name, to surprise or entertain. I must even confess that I have a little conversational bomb which I enjoy dropping from time to time. Well, hardly a bomb, more of a muted trumpet. It consists of a casual remark that I have just signed a contract with the BBC. This occasional event in my life is not really quite so noteworthy as it sounds. A contract with the BBC in my case has little more significance than a letter of acceptance from an editor. Whereas the latter seals a bargain in the manner of a gentlemanly handshake, the contract spells it out in detail. Last time I actually read all the small print.

The background of this particular story was an authentic description of a Greek Island village and some of its characters. What if it were translated into Greek? I asked myself. By the time the day of the first scheduled transmission arrived, I had worked myself into a state akin to first night nerves. It is always an interesting experience to have one's work interpreted, to see it through the hand of an illustrator or to hear the words spoken by an actor. I tuned in with trepidation.

"BBC Radio Four. The time is 10.30, time for Morning Story."

I missed it all. The phone rang, the butcher called, the contractor arrived to pump out the cesspit, a charming customer came to the old forge. She spent a long time deciding to buy a wooden milliner's block. She guessed it was 'real neat' and would be a great Conversation Piece.

I have hard the antiques business described as an incestuous affair. What seems to surprise or even upset many people is the amount of trading which goes on between dealers. In our limited experience we found it to be a very friendly little world with the great majority of fellow dealers most helpful.

There are two main reasons for the volume of trade between dealers. The first is that much of the movement of goods is a sorting out process through which items are eventually channelled to the specialists. From this it follows that if you as a member of the buying public have a specific requirement you can go straight to the specialist for it with good prospects of finding it. It also follows that if you enjoy shopping around or antiquing as our American friends sometimes call it, then there is always the possibility of finding your heart's desire before it has moved right up the scale and reached its full market price.

We sometimes saw our best pieces of pine furniture in London showrooms where the price tag had waxed and grown far. We quickly learned not to be put out by this, in fact, an early lesson was 'to leave something for the next man'. If we had made a reasonable profit and allowed him to do the same, we had also made a friend who would come to us again. And of course that is the other reason for mutual trading, the opportunity to make a profit and the ever-present hope of finding something unrecognised and undervalued. At antiques fairs around the villages and small towns the best part of the day's business is often done in the half hour or so before the public are admitted.

The first time we had a buyer in from the States we wondered what had hit us. He was incidentally sent to us by another dealer with a well established business a couple of miles down the road. The grouping of antique businesses in close proximity is another feature which sometimes puzzles people until it is realised that the great diversity of styles and contents mean that competition in the usual sense hardly exists and is certainly outweighed by the attraction of such concentrations to collectors and Trade buyers.

Milton (call me Chuck) Waggan, the first of our overseas buyers took our breath away. He went round the old forge twice putting his self-adhesive labels on the items he wished to buy, while his assistant recorded them on a 'no-carbon-required' triplicated pad. As sales persons we were entirely redundant. We made coffee and were ready to talk business when he explained the procedure to us!

It is the normal and well established custom in the business to offer a trade discount — this can vary widely though 10% is a good starting point. In the case of sales for export the 15% VAT is recoverable so that one can effect to be offering very favourable terms to such buyers. About a fortnight after Chuck's visit a pantechnicon followed in his footsteps, a cheque would be handed over and the goods carted away to be packed in containers and shipped to the States. In the case of some special items he took instamatic photographs which went on ahead and we were given to understand that some such items were actually sold in the States before they arrived.

Well, that was fine business and very encouraging for the beginners but it also left us feeling somewhat ravaged. Apart from things in our workshop, our entire stock was in the forge and there it was, decimated. We were thrown into something near panic and a desperate need to get out and fill the gaps. And that is one of the many interesting aspects of the business. There is no wholesaler to whom one can telephone an urgent order; finding and buying stock is an entirely individual matter, an exercise which one has to devise and develop in the growing light of experience.

I have already talked about auction sales. We bought far more at sales than anywhere else but never neglected other opportunities. These included other dealers near and far and of distinctly varied descriptions. Bazaars, Jumble Sales, market stalls and builders' skips were never to be passed by for truly one man's trash is another man's treasure. As we became established two other sources opened up. We were invited to inspect and make offers for furniture in private homes and some interesting characters sometimes known as runners appeared on the scene. Neither my wife nor I ever really enjoyed going into people's homes to make offers; we never overcame feelings of embarrassment and in consequence were inclined to offer too much or failed to inspect the piece of furniture in sufficient detail.

Runners is a term in the Trade sometimes applied to the curved rockers on rocking chairs but more often to the variety of individuals who act as go-betweens, offering goods for sale from a third party and selling on commission. Once a good working relationship has been built up with a reputable runner, it can be to everyone's advantage. They seem to know what will interest you and will rarely waste your time. We had one such good friend in Edward. We knew him for about three years before we learned his surname, dealing always in cash until the day he

59

found us with an empty till and graciously accepted a cheque. Of all the contacts I now miss, Edward comes high on the list. He always had a smile, a habit of spitting on cash in his hand and wishing us well.

The aftermath of visits from Chuck and his fellows inevitably prompted a quick trip round some of our favourite hunting-grounds as far afield as Woodbridge and Ipswich and a number of intermediate places such as Debenham. That village had three shops of amazingly disparate character. One entirely beautiful display of art treasures and architectural features, one large furniture establishment and one Aladin's cave.

There was never time on those hectic buying trips to fully enjoy the pleasures of the places. Now that we have retired from the business my wife and I are able to make more leisurely visits. Last summer we meandered up the length of the Deben Valley. The whole 15 miles up to Debenham can be completed on roads so quiet that they make pleasant walking. At Lower Street, Ufford, where I had not been for some years, I was only slightly put out to find belatedly a notice on the door of the village shop which read ''Remember Saturday early closing starts this week''.

Of the two churches, St. Andrews is now declared redundant but the Church of the Assumption in the centre of the village tells a very different story. The building and its contents are a commentary on our history since the time of the Normans, with some comments typically East Anglian, such as the mixed stone and flint work and the 15th century carved oak benches. Our remarks about the 18th century stocks and whipping post were not in accord with so much of today's attitudes to crime and punishment.

Down the street, beyond the Lion we crossed the twin bridges over the clear waters of the Deben and lingered on a grassy bank to watch the inevitable small boys fishing. We speculated on the age of the immense willows beside the water. A swan glided by in solitary regal fashion hardly giving us a glance — it was clearly a superior breed to the shameless beggars we had been feeding earlier down by the tidemark.

The river is a little secretive and hard to reach between here and the old mill at the site of Ash Abbey. There was one heartrending moment on the approach from Ufford when it had seemed inevitable that the rural lane would be eclipsed by the Wickham Market bypass, but all was well and the holiday traffic streamed by a few feet below as we veared off and continued our more leisurely course.

Ash Abbey is one of those delightful places of which one gets fleeting glimpses from the train. I had seen it thus many times before I first managed to reach it on foot. On this return visit it was no less beautiful and we paused happily to watch a competent mother duck supervising a flotilla of thirteen downy chicks.

Below Wickham Market the stream still flows strongly. We grow accustomed to learning that "a mill is recorded on this site in the Domesday Book", and never doubt it for they are the most purposeful of buildings set in absolutely the right places. This pleasant busy little town has undoubtedly been saved from destruction by the building of its bypass. We were charmed by the wickerwork displayed near the bridge and equally by the oven fresh bread available on the other side of the road.

We went on up the valley through the charming hamlets of Easton, Kettleburgh and Cretingham, rarely more than a few yards from the infant Deben, now hardly to be reckoned a river except in winter. Here, as often on our route, the trees met above our heads to form leafy tunnels. There was a better than average display of wayside flowers in this area, perhaps because of the number of dairy herds down in these lush pastures and a more thoughtful approach to spraying chemicals.

Debenham would probably not claim to be the most beautiful village in Suffolk, but no one would deny that there is a certain dishevelled beauty about the place. It certainly has its share of interesting features and can fairly be described as typical of the county. We were happy to call it the goal and the end of our brief journey and did not seek out the actual source of the little trickle beside the street which grows to be the river Deben. As so often happens local opinion is divided on the exact location, but if you say firmly "up Aspall Way" then you can't be wrong.

We had plenty of time to watch wattle fencing being made and to enjoy talking to two charming rush weavers at work. I always find pleasure in watching people at work expecially when employed in ancient crafts still using traditional tools. You will not be surprised that we finished up in the Aladin's cave where I was quite unable to resist three sets of goat collars and chains and a wooden box full of cobblers clobber.

We have also had time to revisit Woolpit. In the continuous quest for new sources our 'chief buyer' had discovered a regular auction sale in the village hall. It became one of her most favoured haunts as the people who were running it were unfailingly charming and helpful. In addition to that she felt that she was not on strange ground as in the course of one long hot homeless summer we had spent some time on the edge of that village.

I still recall waking on our first morning there and wondering where I was. The dawn chorus was in full session around us and I remembered that the night before we had parked our caravan alongside an extensive hawthorn thicket. Before I fell asleep again I had identified about a dozen different bird songs but was sadly conscious of the absence of the cuckoo. The next time I woke it was time to fetch a pint of milk and collect a paper from one of the shops in the village.

We had not come to Woolpit entirely by chance. An enchanting picture had something to do with it. A picture with white plastered houses, weatherboarding and small-paned windows; an irregular tiled roofline with an uncharacteristic Suffolk church beyond.

There was a shadow in the foreground of the picture which seemed to indicate a market cross or similar structure which turned out to be the pump and well of remembrance for Queen Victoria set at the junction of the three roads. The fact that there are but three roads gives the centre of the village an immediate advantage, taking from it the almost inevitable squareness usually produced by crossroads.

We hadn't immediately visited the church, we waited until the Sunday morning. This was an excellent move. Although the exceptionally beautiful wood carvings of the roof timbers and many other features make a vist at any time worthwhile, to have joined an unexpectedly large congregation for choral communion added an extra dimension. This was no museum piece viewed to the accompaniment of hushed whispers and the clop of hard heel on flagstones, but the living heart of a small community, warm in the May sunshine and cheerful with the sound of singing.

It was by chance that we found ourselves encamped on the fringe of a curiously contorted strip of land at the edge of the village. No great detective work was called for to surmise that this had been a brickfield and one of our local informants (at the Swan) soon filled in our lack of knowledge about Woolpit Whites. These bricks enjoyed quite a spell of popularity though, colourwise, not standing up too well to the test of time. This may sound a strange thing to say of them considering that there is some evidence that the Romans made bricks here and that production continued on and off until just after the Second World War.

It is thought likely that the second half of the name of the village derived from these claypits, and alternatives are offered for the first half. This may have come from the wolves of Saxon times or from Ulf, a onetime local chieftain.

Arriving at Woolpit from Worstead I had mistakenly assumed from the name a strong connection in the past with the wool trade. Although there is a house in the village called Weavers, next door to Little Spinners, there is no evidence of any large involvement in the trade beyond the local needs.

No-one is now likely to settle this academic point, nor to throw any new light on the curious local legend of the two green children. The account tells of a young boy and girl, both clothed in green and with skin to match, who emerged from a pit one harvest-time and were found wandering in the fields. The villagers were, not surprisingly, rather apprehensive but took them in charge and imprisoned them in the village. Neither child would eat the food offered to them till be chance the boy was offered and accepted some green peas.. From then on they both took nourishment and tried to answer the many questions put to them. However, their explanations of whence they had come were never fully understood. The boy continued to weaken and died. The girl grew strong as she got used to the food available. Her skin grew to a natural colour and it is said that she eventually married a young man from Kings Lynn.

In our continuing search for a new home we were offered the former butcher ship in the village. A pleasant coincidence this as the shop is right in the centre of that picture which first attracted us to the place. My wife drew my attention to the fact that the presence or absence of an active butcher's shop in a village is a good indicator of the life and prosperity of the community, and this could be taken as a case in point. Woolpit, one might say, has been twice by-passed in recent times. First when major improvements were made to remove the turnpike and its growing traffic load to the north of the village, and now again as the new dual carriageway sweeps majestically past. Heavy lorries, transporters and a procession of traffic roar past the severed arteries which used to lead into the village streets. An uneasy air of relative tranquillity descends on communities thus cut off. At first it is entirely delightful; the rumble and dust is stilled; the corners of buildings are no longer nipped off; pavements no more eroded; it becomes safe once again for people to move about.

But in such reborn peace there lurks another danger. The life and motive force which created the village may also depart, like the young people, to the towns. Preservation orders can help to retain architectural merit and visual pleasures, but laws alone can neither make us love our neighbours nor preserve life itself.

I like to remember Woolpit by the words on the memorial well:

"Every place has water, light and air and God's abounding grace.
All noblest things are still the commonplace."

We love the village still but feel that we were right in rejecting it as a site for our new enterprise in Antiques.

The Village Pump - Woolpit

(Photograph courtesy of Images Publications from the book "Images of Suffolk").

LOT 6
A Gaggle of Geese

We missed Harry and Hilda. It was quiet around the cottage and in the orchard. A moorhen's cry echoed under the bridge but there was no answering sound from beneath the willows. Harry and Hilda were wrapped in their plastic shrouds in a cold corner of the deep freeze. Of course it had been a mistake to give them names and to allow them to become such close friends. We had never intended to become so involved or to form anything other than a temporary acquaintanceship.

They had joined us soon after we arrived at our new home; March goslings just old enough to feed on the new grass. Our plan was that they would look after the orchard while we put our home in order. By the time autumn came the writing would be on the wall for them as for great numbers of "Michaelmas geese". September 29th is by long tradition the end of the goose cycle, which closely follows the growing period of grass. it was a good plan well executed and that was just how it felt at the end — like the execution of two old friends. We told ourselves not to be stupid and sentimental and to think of the money we would save by not bying a turkey at Christmas.

Down at the stream even the water seemed to have lost its vitality. Harry and Hilda succeeded in making their absence something positive which didn't lessen as the weeks went by. Into this void came three distinguished Chinese geese. Well, they didn't exactly come but the manner of their being brought was entirely unpremediated and was attended by some humour. It was William's turn to attend the weekly Wednesday market. Being a warm and pleasant day he first bought himself a haircut and then, perhaps deciding after all that it wasn't so warm, he bought himself a hat. Having time in hand before the start of the furniture auction he took a walk round the poultry section, saw this splendid cob and brought it home. Not a profitable outing but we all agreed that it had been an opportunity not to be missed.

Now a very odd thing came about, for although this aristocrat was clearly not destined for the pot, he did not instantly acquire a name as Harry had done. We installed him on the grassy slope beside the stream, gave him a lavish supply of litter in the sleeping quarters and a couple of handfuls of barley sweepings for his supper. Nothing we did pleased him or made him feel at ease. He took little interest in food and spent most of the next six days pacing the wire perimeter like a demented P.O.W.

The following Wednesday it was my wife's turn to go to market. She too visited the poultry section and by great good fortune was able to bid for and get two young Chinese geese — "thought to be female". Once again there were no further thoughts of buying furniture; the problems of securing and transporting two bedraggled but lively geese were sufficient. They arrived home in the back of the estate car wrapped in blankets, having proved on the journey to be distracting and quite useless as co-drivers.

We introduced the new arrivals to the cob. The vendor and the auctioneer may have doubted their feminity; the cob had no doubts on the subject. There were great splashings in the brook and soon the happy trio were preening themselves on the grass outside our workshop. Life was all domestic bliss from then on, with no more perimeter pacing.

I freely confess that we spent a lot of time watching them when we might have been working. They always seemed to look at their best in the late afternoons with the sunlight reflecting upwards from the rippling waters of the brook. After an extended preening session they stood there in all their beauty and elegance. Their main plumage is snowy white. It sets off to perfection the varying shades of brown which start as a dark stripe on the back of their heads and run down almost to their tails. Cheeks, throats, and breasts are graduations of fawn. Brown appears again on their flight feathers. it is no wonder that the all white variety are often mistaken for swans as they have elegance on water and regal dignity on land.

We were absurdly surprised when eggs suddenly appeared. There was no messing about with misshapen or undersized eggs like pullets but a straight succession of 6 ¼ oz golden yolked beauties. I don't believe that they even considered the nesting boxes. They seem quite happy to lay in the straw in the far corner of their sleeping quarters, but they did behave like naughty children at bed-time if we left the soiled straw too long before providing a fresh supply.

We had to shut them up in their fox-proof house at night. When released in the mornings they burst on the world like children into a playground, an all-singing, all-dancing gaggle, but they soon regained their composure and took their places on stage for the day's amphibious performance.

The geese and the old dog which we had at the that time lived together in a state of armed neutrality. All had free range in the stream and most

of the garden. Only the vegetable plot was wired off forbidden territory. We learned to garden with geese which in the end means growing only those plants which they don't care for, flowering shrubs and trees. They helped with the grass and also earned their keep as night watchmen, protesting loudly against intruders even when secured in their night-quarters. They became quite one of the attractions of the place and even if they did go for a few people, I don't believe that we ever lost a customer.

The old dog had rather less to commend him, yet even in his old age I still found it possible to envy one thing, his sense of smell. He could still scent and point to a sitting bird and clearly received a Babel of messages over the air which failed to reach me.

When we walked in places such as Thetford Chase or Salthouse Heath we sometimes became aware of a faint insidious sweetness in the air, cloying and rather nauseous, something dead in the bracken or heather. If the dog found it he rolled in it, even if he failed to eat it, so we whistled him in and increased our pace. We left the offensiveness being for nature to deal with, while we breathed more deeply the scent of sunwarmed pines or stepped towards the coast and inhaled the clean air over the saltings.

When we were similarly assaulted in our own gardens, a quick search, a spade and a decent burial dealt conlusively with the matter. When pestilence entered our home we suffered.

The first time we detected the telltale whiff we tracked it down to the airing cupboard. it was our own fault really as we had been putting down poison for the mice. One perisher had crawled irretrievably under the hot tank to die. The cupboard had to be emptied. Fortunately the warm situation speeded decomposition and dehydration so our own life returned to normal in about two weeks. It was not the reason why we sold the house and moved.

A thatch, such as we had on the cottage, is not only a thing of beauty, it is also inclined to become a preoccupation and, like ourselves, to need more loving care and attention as the years go by. It is maddening to lie in bed and see sparrows gently destroying the roof over ones head. Even worse is when the vermin who try to inhabit it, who perversely destroy it, are inconsiderate enough to die in it.

The first time this happened we took some time to track it down and dispose of the corpse. It was not an entirely profitless exercise as I greatly enjoyed the time spent with a powerful electric torch between joists and rafters studying the thatchers' craft from the inside.

On the next occasion the first hint of trouble reached us outside the study door. We looked reproachfully at the dog, studied our boots and said nothing. Next day, the smell was inescapable and comment unavoidable. It might well have been a case of "let well alone and it will go away" but it didn't give that impression and got steadily worse.

I am not sure exactly how smell travels. In his book "Mr Perrin and Mr Trail" Hugh Walpole writes of mutton stew on Tuesdays. He vividly describes the damp greasy odour creeping along the passage from the kitchen, seeping through cracks above and below the door to envelop the assembled company as they stood waiting for Latin Grace to be said. Any one of us who went to that same school will confirm the accuracy of his description.

Something similar now happened. The smell spread obtrusively yet at times elusively round the cottage. it seemed in some mysterious way to follow the hot water pipes, to settle in layers like mist on the moor or to pile up in corners.

The second day the offensiveness was carried into our bedroom. We passed a fitful night and next day made a strategic withdrawal to the caravan. the middle of March is not time for such action but we had to open all doors and windows of the cottage and carry out our continued search in woollen gloves and windcheaters.

We speak of 'a measurer of success', but how do we measure success? We found and removed the odiferous rat but at what a price! It cost us two strained backs, moving all the bedroom furniture, lifting the carpet and removing three floor-boards before our efforts were rewarded with the smell of victory. Throughout the period of emergency the old dog remained aloof and disinterested. He wasn't any help at all but nor was he of any special hindrance.

This talk of offensive smells reminds me that some years ago I developed a strange longing for a set of cane drain rods. I knew that neat and prudent people like my brother-in-law always had a set handy in their tool shed; a sort of insurance policy, like the fire extinguisher in his garage, the first aid kit in the caravan or the shovel and bag of sand in the car boot during the winter.

Perhaps I thought of them as a status symbol; an adult version of my Scout's knife. I never had met that proverbial horse with a stone in its hoof, but preparedness is a positive virtue. It was certainly not that I had any actual need of a set.

At our first house, in Pakefield, the rainwater from the slates soaked quickly and easily into the sandy soil. Our other drains ran immediately under the wooden fence, following a former right of way through our neighbour's property. I recall only one minor malfunction in all the years that we lived there and that was clearly our neighbour's problem and not ours.

Then we moved to an old farmhouse near Worstead. It was bereft of its land but retained a large walled garden, outbuildings of which we still think wistfully and a small triangular pightle beyond the cart sheds into which it was thought that the drains passed.

In fact they did no such thing. With the help of a Dowser we unearthed a magnificent private drainage system of early Victorian splendour. Two main subterranean caverns were bricked and arched; their in-flow and out-fall arrangements more worthy of an ornamental grotto. We diverted most of the rainwater from our pantile roofs to the garden area, refurbished the underground system and established a balance with nature which served us faultlessly until we moved to The Old Forge.

It is not until one lives with a thatched roof or dubious drains that one gives such matters much thought. To arrange troughing in an attempt to catch the waters from a thatch is an unsatisfactory business, rarely efficient and always unsightly. On one side of our cottage such water fell on a concrete apron and ran to the orchard. No great interest there. On the other side it disappeared into a culvert and re-emerged to join the stream. Our more serious drains were contained within a system which required expert servicing at regular intervals by a man from the District Authority.

Not long after we moved in my wife started attending regular auction sales. One day she arrived home with an artistic collection made up of a roll of roofing felt (only slightly damaged) which we needed for the roof of the goosehouse, an interesting bundle of sticks and umbrellas and a complete set of drain rods. They were a fine set such as I had long wanted.

I cleared a space in the workshop and set the bundle ready for instant action. Once more I was prepared. It felt like a re-affirmation of my Scout's Promise. It was something of an anticlimax when time passed and nothing went wrong with the drains. Someone told me that the canes need wetting from time to time to keep them supple. I never got around to doing that and they gathered dust for two years.

Then one morning, after a night of rain, my wife said to me, "You'll have to do something about that drain!" My moment of glory was upon me. The water was flowing down the garden path, making quite a pretty cascade at the three steps and out of the gateway into the lane.

I was out there in a flash, rods at the ready, and straight into action. Twisting and thrusting I had eight lengths up the culvert before making contact with the obstruction. What it was I shall never know. It felt soft and was undoubtedly nauseous. It came down the pipe with a throaty plop and a rush of water which nearly took me downstream with it.

Flushed with triumph I started to withdraw my rods. In my folly and ignorance I twisted in a lefthand direction, like taking out a corkscrew. the rods disengaged, leaving four sections somewhere between the stream and the cottage. That was the moment when Ben arrived. He took in the whole situation at a glance and pronounced his verdict: "The trouble is", he said, "you aren't up to it!"

When we had asked in the village shop if there was a local plumber, they said, "Yes, everyone knows Ben." If Ben wasn't to be found in his workshop behind the pink cottage at the end of the street, there was a good chance of finding him in the snug at the Cross Keys. If he wasn't there, then one of his cronies would be sure to know where he was working. All this we were told in the shop. We followed the pleasant trail which eventually led us to the yard behind Jim's farmhouse. There was Ben, lost in thought, contemplating an old lead pump bolted to the wall.

"Ha!" Ben had said, "I thought you'd soon be looking for me. You've just moved into Forge Cottage, haven't you, and you want me to do something about that cistern of yours which you can't make flush. I'll be round fuss thing in the morning for sure."

Exerience had taught me to beware of that expression "for sure" and to paraphrase it as "possibly, if I don't forget or if nothing else of greater importance turns up." But on that first occasion, Ben was there and had caught me as my triumph had turned to shame.

"I didn't really need to come at all', he announced. "There ain't nothing seriously wrong with that cistern of yours, it's all a matter of approach. What you've got to do is seem unconcerned and then give it a quick, sharp jab when it's not expecting you.'' He proved his point by demonstration, accepted a cup of coffee and departed, leaving us with a whole new range of study opening up in psychological aspects of mechanical contrivances.

As time passed and we became a part of the social round in the village, we learned that nearly everyone had an after dinner story to tell about Ben and his activities. Anne, the Colonel's wife, delighted in telling her story about the new wash basin which Ben had installed in their cloakroom. The first time the Colonel went to use it, hot water emerged from the tap marked 'cold' and vice versa. The restraint with which he summoned Ben to rectify the error was, we understood, a model of decorum for us all. Ben actually put things right in three minutes flat by changing over the tops of the taps, a much speedier solution than in the case of Miss Love at Rose Cottage who complained of hot flushes after the installation of a new cistern in her bathroom.

I don't intend to parade all my family before you, just a couple of aunts who have some bearing on the story and a few mentions in passing as other members crop up.

My wife and I have searched our family trees for fame and found none. Distinction yes but neither fame nor infamy. At only one point can we detect even a rubbing of shoulder with notoriety. That was in an unlikely person of her Great Aunt Fanny.

G.A.F.'s grave is only a few feet from that of Rose Harsent, the girl who was found murdered in the kitchen of Providence Home, Peasenhall, on June 1st 1902. After the police investigations were completed, Fanny who was a near neighbour, was asked to help clear up the bloody mess. Family history relates that the shock of what she saw brought on diabetes from which she died not many years later.

Those of us now in our sixties and seventies were a generation blessed with a fair proliferation of aunts and uncles from large Victorian families.

I wish that you had known my Aunt Ethel. I admired her tremendously and felt saddened and cheated when she died. Perhaps because she had no children of her own she was a specially indulgent aunt. She and my uncle often took me out for a day's sailing on their cruiser Harrier, which was usually based near Horning.

In my eyes Harrier was the most beautiful boat on the Norfolk Broads. Built in the early nineteen hundreds by the Norfolk Navigation Company, gaff rigged, clinker built and with most distinctive 'Viking' bows.

I was well instructed in the pleasures of sailing. Not cut-throat competition stuff, but the pleasurable appreciation of leisurely sailing with occasional excitement offered by the moods of wind and water. There was always time to absorb the beauties of Broadland. I am not sure that the word ecology had been invented. I learned about flora and fauna and to respect other people's interests. Vocabulary too was gently instilled in me; such lovely words as Rond, Quant, Dydle, Luff and Jibe.

In the course of time I graduated to being lent the boat for holidays. I quickly came to regard motor cruisers in a truly Arthur Ransome manner as a lower form of life, expecially the Hullabaloos.

At that time sail still just predominated on the Broads. Aunt Ethel, I noted, was always quick to recognise the burgee being flown on other sailing craft. If it was a club rather than a boatyard it usually took her only a short time to identify the owner.

It was rather similar when she took me to Fakenham or Hethersett races. She knew all about racing colours and it seemed to me that she knew just about everyone in the country. You could say that she needed an acolite trailing along behind her to pick up the names she dropped.

One odd foible I recall was her fixed rule to place a bet on the first horse which she saw on the day. I am unable to report the financial results of this slightly eccentric approach.

She also took me to meets of the Dunston Harriers. There was a certain formality to those occasions and Aunt Ethel never failed to offer instruction on good manners and correct procedures. Using the right words was all part of this. For example, dogs were hounds, a jockey wore silks, boats were made fast, while a sure knowledge of port and starboard was absolutely basic.

It may have been from Aunt Ethel that I caught a mild infection of her name dropping habit. Quite a harmless habit really if not allowed to run to excess. Who can be blamed for wishing to improve his image through association with the good and the great? You know the sort of thing I mean. A story about visiting Welney Wildfowl Trust is enhanced by the fact that one happened to share a hide with Sir Peter Scott. An account of some events in Malta is enlivened by mention of the name of the Admiral who was involved or the name of the General for whom one arranged a duck shoot in North Africa. The fact that the beaters were armed with Tommy guns to make the ducks get up off the lake to be shot at fades into insignificance.

For a good many years now I have been able to derive quiet pleasure from being able to drop the words "My Editor". It has proved quite useful sometimes in helping along a sticky conversation. More recently came the day when I could mention in passing "My Producer at Pebble Mill".

One of my unfulfilled ambitions has been to have a book published and to be able to refer casually to "My Publishers". I could see the book quite clearly in my mind's eye; a rather handsome volume, hard-backed, and with gold leaf embossed on the spine. It might just possibly have a dust jacket, certainly a profusion of sketches to illustrate the text. It would have a good feel, just the right weight for comfortable reading and would certainly be printed on good quality paper in a clean clear typeface. It would in fact be a product of which Aunt Ethel would have been pleased. She might even have dropped our name occasionally. "My Dear, of course I know the author, my nephew, actually."

The other aunt I must mention was rather eccentric, well, between you and me she was quite potty. Anyhow, I remember her with nothing but pleasure, although I actually saw very little of her. She was my widower uncle's second wife and when that all happened I was away in India. I gather that nobody really noticed that she was potty until my uncle inconsiderately and precipitiously made her a widow.

Almost immediately Aunt Dorothy sold her home and moved. This surprised no-one and it wasn't until she moved again, and then a third time, that eyebrows started to be raised. In all, she moved eighteen times, though never going outside Norfolk, which I personally regard as a point very much to her credit.

She had a theory that she made money every time she moved. I understand that this was based on the theoretical savings she made by selecting houses which cost a few thousand pounds less than the ones she would really have liked to buy. Not very sound economics, too much like giving away potatoes to save losing money on every bag sold.

It wasn't just a matter of houses either. There was a string of curious activities into which she threw herself with short bursts of excessive zeal. One of the earliest of these was keeping donkeys. A laudable enterprise, you might say, giving a good home to one or two donkeys rescued from distressful circumstances. So it could have been if it had not grown out of all proportion, necessitating at least two moves to pastures new and even larger, and ultimately out-running her enthusiasm.

She managed to dispose of the donkeys and moved to a small-holding to specialise in growing melons. At least, that was the stated intention, which required considerable outlay on Dutch lights and the construction of solar pits. My information is that she never did produce a melon but went to stay with a friend in Bournemouth at the critical time, forgetting to make any arrangements for the watering of the plants.

Soon after this fiasco, Dolly called me on the 'phone. It was, I believe, the first time she had ever done so. Would I like to have my grandfather's grandfather clock? She was moving to a little cottage near Dickleburgh in which there was no room tall enough for the long case clock. If I wanted it, and I couldn't accept fast enough, she would leave it on the veranda as the moving van was just about to depart.

My wife and I jumped into our Ford van and set off, like Little Noddy, at top speed. We found the clock as promised. It was in pieces. We collected them up, took them home, put them together and it went. I am sure that Benjamin Sudlow, who built the clock at Great Yarmouth in 1764 would have been just as delighted as we were.

In the course of the next twelve years, Dolly moved on from cottage to houses to flats and bungalows and finally to a private hotel. She had kept a monkey, budgerigars, Siamese cats and, to the last, some very smelly dogs, not entirely housetrained. During the same period, we moved home three times — yes, I know, but in our case, the moves were dictated by the need to be near my place of work. On the third move, Benjamin (the clock) suffered some damage and refused to go. Almost simultaneously, Dolly died.

Some long time later, we took Benjamin to a clockmaker. The estimate for repair which we were given so shook us that we did nothing about it and were some weeks before we even went to fetch him sadly home. He remained reproachfully silent.

The solicitors took eight years to finalise Dolly's affairs. When they did so, I found myself to be one of eleven residual legatees to benefit from my uncle's Will. The sum of money which I received paid for Benjamin's restoration. He keeps good time, strikes mellifluously and is still kept level by a folded cigarette card which pictures a Bedlington Terrier — a breed much favoured by my aunt.

Benjamin, the long case clock, is still with us. He, unlike many of our possessions, has survived all our moves and financial crises. There are two opposing forces at work when you deal in antiques and bygones. On the one hand there is a great desire to keep the most beautiful and interesting object while on the other hand the need to pay the grocer's bill can bring one to part with cherished items. We often dealt with the first of these problems of keeping things and enjoying them for a period of time and then letting someone else have the pleasure. The sets of chairs which passed through our dining room would reach from here to the end of the lane. They were improved by the loving care they received and their value more than held up with inflation.

In an odd sort of way my next-door-neighbour reminds me of my Grandfather. Perhaps it is his upright carriage and direct manner.

"I'm going to try my hand at some plastering this weekend," he said recently. "Can you lend me the right clothes?" Now I'm not what you would call a sharp dresser, but I do have two boiler suits, one white and one blue. One or other usually seems suitable for most of the jobs I do around the place. Also, now I come to think of it, I have a selection of headgear for various activities such as house painting, tree felling or gardening in the rain. I use a mustard yellow apron when brewing or working in the kitchen and a hessian one when doing a stint of rush-seating or carpentry. Until now it really had not struck me that I dress up for jobs.

If I thought about it at all, I would consider that the right clothes for a job are just as necessary as the right tools. For example, the blue boilersuit has a pocket for a two foot ruler and a handy one for a pencil, while the white one has always got a useful piece of wiping rag and some sandpaper stowed in it. The hip pocket is ideal for a painter's duster. The kangaroo pouch of my hessian apron actually holds all the tools needed for rushwork, so they are always to hand as required.

If, indeed, "the apparel oft proclaims the man", then I suppose that I am proclaimed as one of varied interests, most of them of a practical nature. In contrast, I think of my paternal grandfather. He was a solicitor. I see him always in my mind's eye as the epitome of a city gentleman. I do not recall ever seeing him dressed other than in a dark suit, with highly polished shoes, a discreet amount of white lawn handkerchief showing at his breast pocket and more often than not, a carnation at his lapel.

As children we were much overawed by his appearance and military manner. His moustache and speech alike were clipped and precise. He was clearly ready to draw up a will at short notice or to convey a property (marked pink on the attached plan). Indeed his precision and fastidiousness were oddly in contrast with the dusty gloom of his offices in Opie Street. It was this latter state which caused me at an early age to reject the possibility of joining the family firm of solicitors. We can all look back on missed opportunities and this was an early one on my part.

To study the history of occupational costume is in effect to study social history. One of the many fascinating aspects is the way in which working clothes evolved from comparative uniformity in the remoter past to the distinctive dress of individual trades, and have now reverted to almost total anonymity. Such distinctions as remain are vestigial only and usually associated with status symbols rather than any practical purpose.

Even the term "white collar worker", which at one time aptly distinguished clerical from manual, is already as outmoded as the stiffly starched white collars.

No one who remembers wearing starched collars, especially as I did at school, laments their demise. Something which passed with them, unsung and hardly remembered, is that whole area of laundering which was devoted to the 'dressing' of collars. I am not sure if it should be described as a labour or an art. Certainly much skill went into the processes of washing, starching, blocking, polishing and curling. Nor do we now have resort to goffering irons to produce the frills of the 'easycare' fabrics now used for choirboys ruffs. Several of those goffering irons passed through our hands at the Old Forge.

There are many such instances where changes in fashion have resulted in the loss of whole industries formerly devoted to the production and servicing of the items involved. Perhaps few more striking than the hat trade. Despite brave efforts in advertising ("If you want to get ahead, get a hat"), the current decline in the wearing of hats, except for ritual or ceremonial occasions, is almost absolute. This too has produced a fall-out of interesting bygones for collectors.

Strangely, it was in the field of headgear that disposables were first pioneered. Paper hats came into use by tradesmen in the early eighteen hundreds and by mid century, when paper was becoming cheaper, there are well authenticated records of at least two dozen trades which affected the wearing of paper hats. These include Printers, Goldbeaters and Warpscourers as well as the much better known Carpenter, recorded for posterity in 'Alice in Wonderland'.

Despite its former widespread use, I have failed in my best efforts to find someone who can show me how to fold those traditional square paper hats. I am reliably informed that if I care to re-visit Rome, I may yet be in time to find some building workers who have lost neither the habit nor the art. As a dealer in bygones I would have to classify such items a 'paper ephemera'.

I should mention that the apparel of my other grandfather was an entirely different cup of tea. If the tweed of his suits and in particular his Norfolk jacket proclaimed a country gentleman, they did no more than speak the truth. He was one of the most gentle men I have known.

Like his father before him, he was the village doctor and for me he has always personified the very best in the tradition of a country practitioner. Memories of him too have often crept into my mind as medical memorabilia is a rich field for collectors.

He always wore a gold watch, which was as much a tool of his trade as the stethoscope in his pocket. He had an aura of quiet competence which never seemed to leave him and which inspired confidence in his patients as well as in a small grandson.

Now that my neighbour's mockery has opened my eyes to the fact that I am a 'dresser-up', I can admit that I have long coveted a Norfolk jacket exactly on the lines of the ones my grandfather wore. It would be absolutely right for many of my activities. The only thing which puts me off is the thought that perhaps my neighbour would want to borrow it every time he takes his dog for a walk and wears his deerstalker hat.

We were in trouble when we moved into Forge Cottage. We thought there was no ceiling high enough to accommodate Benjamin until we discovered the lean-to entrance porch gave us a full 78 inches and we were delighted to find the silhouette on the wall of the previous owner's clock where he had painted round it.

Another unexpected difficulty in the cottage was finding wall space for our favourite pictures. Not only was the light rather poor with small leaded windows and exposed timbers, those delights of deceptive house agents, considerably reduced potential wall space. Drastic pruning was necessary. Some we put aside for sale in the shop. Some, after much debate, we decided to put into a saleroom and I was elected for the job.

No one who knows me would expect to find me enthusing about a day in London. Of course I was lucky enough to strike things just right; a misty morning giving way to full spring sunshine and the Capital looking its best.

I zipped up to town on the Inter City Service, and if I begin to sound like a B.R. press release it can only be that everything turned out just the way they claim it to be. The surprising fact is that I positively enjoyed the journey, right from the moment when I bought my ticket over a counter instead of from that faceless gnome who used to hide through a little hatchway.

Almost every East Anglian must surely have his own associations with a train journey to London, be it the memory of a trip to the Cup Final, a wedding, or maybe a successful day at the sales. I used to return to school each term along this line and at later dates it was my route to join the army and for forays further afield.

The smooth ride was even more soporific than the well remembered rhythm of "tak tak tackity tack", but the changing panorama of Spring displayed at speed was full enough of interest to keep anyone awake.

My business in town was brief and successfully concluded. My visit to a famous saleroom — an evocative phrase which I had not previously acted out was in itself a rewarding experience. The almost reverent quiet and stillness made it seem like a visit to a shrine devoted to the worship of Mammon. One might say that it is just that.

I had a sneaking sensation of treachery as I parted with a painting by one of the Norwich School, but the memory of it is deeply etched and I am sure that it will give pleasure to its new owner. It seemed entirely appropriate that my package was wrapped with a copy of the Eastern Daily Press and tied with binder twine; facts which were not wasted on the charming staff at the saleroom, one of whom was a native of Suffolk.

With time in hand and the sun now pleasantly warm I decided to walk back from Belgravia. A sentimental walk it turned out to be, surprising me with the number of memories roused.

Green Park was looking its beautiful best with flower and foliage a good ten days ahead of home. I was delighted to rediscover how one can bask in a pool of green tranquillity with traffic noises swirling round the fringe.

Piccadilly Circus I thought tawdry and dirty compared with the bright lights of memory; safety railings add nothing to the visual pleasures. The Haymarket presented me with the customary lure of window-shopping outside the lost property shop and an irresistible dive into the Design Centre.

And so down to Trafalgar Square. I looked at Nelson, cocked hat almost in the mist, with something of a proprietorial air; a son of Norfolk occupying the finest site in the capital. The fountains sparkled, pigeons were fed, cameras clicked, traditions were being well observed and I even heard a few people speaking English.

On then towards the Victoria Embankment. The hard pavements were beginning to hurt my feet in my city shoes, so I gave Parliament Square a miss and headed for an old friend of mine — The Discovery. Once in those far-off days when I was a Sea Scout I had the pleasure of sleeping aboard this piece of floating history. Pleasant proportions and lines give little indication of her massive strength and ability to resist the pressures of antarctic ice. When one was snugged down in a box bunk there was about 26 inches of solid timbers to keep out the noise of the trams screeching along the Embankment. One was in a good position to appreciate the beauties of English oak, pitchpine, Honduras mahogany, elm and greenheart.

I dragged myself away to climb up on to the new Waterloo bridge. Even though it was the wrong one, so to speak, it certainly gave a view which was "touching in its majesty". The tide was slopping out fairly swiftly and my thoughts moved on quickly from Wordsworth to A.P. Herbert and I felt the quickening of a never too deeply dormant desire

78

to be off down to the sea in ships.

Time, like the tide, was now running out so I looked for a No. 11 bus to take me back past St. Pauls and through the City to Liverpool Street.

It hardly needs to be said that for me the best part of any journey is the end of the return half. When I come home from London by car I usually start to breathe more freely round about Royston; my heart lifts to the swell of the sweeping acres of the chalk uplands and the fine stands of beech. When coming by train the cavern of Liverpool Street Station is the threshold of home, for all those outward journeys undertaken with dread or doubt have had their counterparts of joyful return. All the names on the train departure indicator are familiar and even a few faces are recognisable.

So there was never any doubt that I would enjoy that part of the day. I sat back and rested my feet, watching the fields flick by, punctuated by tantalising fragments of other people's lives as seen from a passing train, and the not unpleasing thoughts of one of my Grandfather's pictures being turned into cash.

Three of the pictures which survived that shake out hang on the wall beside my desk as I write. The first, by the Suffolk artist Keith Pilling, is of the old forge as he saw it, before it was re-thatched. It shows a very ragged 'Thelwellian' building much in need of the thorough grooming which it later received. The second is not really a picture, but the delightful printed billhead, dated September 30th, 1925. It is an account for six months' work done for Mr. Smith of Kiln Farm by W. E. Goldsmith who was at that date operating the forge and living in the cottage which is now our home.

Pride of place is taken by the third picture. The age-darkened maple frame holds a print of "Shoeing" by Sir Edwin Lanseer. It was not all that easily come by. The first one which we saw such as this was in another country antiques shop not two miles away. At that time we were still negotiating for possession of the old forge. When the legal processes had ground themselves slowly to completion and we were the proud owners, we went back to buy the print. By that time, of course, it had gone.

The next copy we saw was in the saleroom at Aylsham. We were not the only contenders and although we very much wanted it, the price went up beyond what we considered reasonable. Our son William eventually secured the copy which now hangs on the wall beside me. He did a deal with a man who had bought a mixed lot of prints which included "A Sopwith Pup", artist unknown, "Bubbles" by Sir Joshua Reynolds and this print.

A tale, you might say, of prevarication. Lanseer himself was one of

79

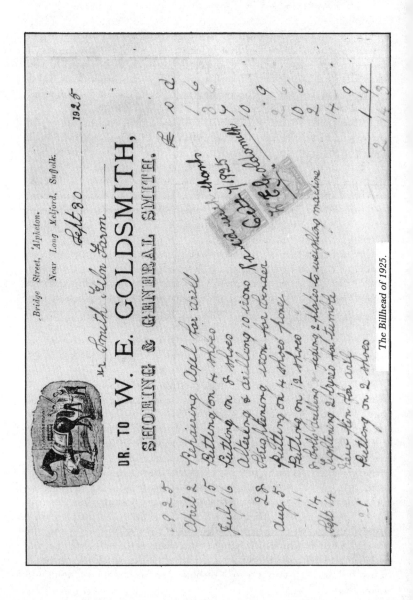

The Billhead of 1925.

80

the greatest of prevaricators. He developed it almost to an art form and the story of how he eventually painted the picture of the bay mare is a case in point.

Betty, the mare, belonged to Jacob Bell who, in common with many another of his generation, wanted a painting of this, his favourite. The plan was to have her painted with foal at foot, so Betty was put to a stallion. In due course the foal arrived and once it was reasonably stable on its feet, it was considered that the ideal moment had arrived for the painting to be executed.

Lanseer had been kept fully informed of progress and at this point he was urgently requested to attend and perform the work. In spite of freqent reminders he failed to do so and the colt quickly outgrew its mother. Jacob Bell did not give up easily. The apologies which he received from Lanseer and the artist's assurances that such a thing would not happen again encouraged him to make a second attempt. Accordingly the services of the stallion were again called for and a second foal was produced. Unfortunately the news brought more prevarication and excuses and the 'foal' was finally sold as a four-year-old still without being painted with its mother.

A year later Lanseer visited Bell, with whom he remained somewhat surprisingly on friendly terms. He saw and admired Betty, immediately wishing to paint her! As no foal could be produced at short notice, the donkey was bought in, the scene set in the smithy, and the remarkable painting produced.

In spite of the fact that Lanseer was a great favourite of Queen Victoria, who thought him "certainly the cleverest artist there is", he was by no means without his critics. "Shoeing" was no exception. Ruskin himself seems to have reversed his earlier praise of Lanseer's work and led the chorus of niggling criticism. This was not confined to the treatment of the subject but to the subject itself. They scoffed at the thought of the mare standing unhaltered to be shod, though in fact Betty customarily did so. They laughed at the positioning of her leading offside foot, but to stand thus, with little weight on her toe, was another of her peculiarities. So too was the near presence of the donkey; an inseparable companion in her advancing years. The critics dismissed the whole scene as 'an inanity'.

I make no claim to be critic or connoissuer. The bay mare looked very much at home in our old forge. It took but little imagination to hear the ring of the anvil, the creak of the bellows and to catch an elusive whiff of hot metal on hoof.

LOT 7
Greenfingers

A cutting from the Eastern Evening News dated 2 April 1941 reminds me that my grandfather was a keen gardener. "Though advanced years now prevent him from serving his country in the army, as he did in the last war, Colonel S. Garerd Hill, at the age of 81, is among the Diggers for Victory ... he keeps going a ten-rod allotment not far from his home ... His erect and neat figure and buoyant step still witness his early military training and he can do a brisk walk of several miles without the least fatigue."

I have to admit that even with several years in hand I don't measure up well to such an example. I can't even claim with honesty to be any better than a reluctant gardener. My wife, however, is indefatigable and I am always ready to offer encouragement and admire the works of others. I enjoy visiting gardens with my wife. She does a fair imitation of a humming-bird, moving from bloom to bloom as if absorbing nectar and murmuring incantations like a Latin mass. She has an eye for detail, colour and new varieties for which she can usually produce the proper botanical name as well as the common one.

It sometimes happens that when we are on holiday or have a free Sunday, we look at the list of gardens open for our pleasure in aid of the Red Cross or other charities and set out for another botanical beanfeast. Over the years we have had some rare treats. My preference is for the larger works of Capability Brown and those followers of his style; improving nature's own arrangements with the use of water, landscaping and the careful planting and choice of trees; the creation of vistas, the emphasising of individual specimens and sometimes even creating the illusion of greater expanses than really exist. Stourhead, in Wiltshire, immediately comes to my mind as an example.

We have enjoyed the truly great and some quite modest gardens. Rather surprisingly, we were enticed up to London in order to visit a garden. A Fellow of the Royal Horticultural Society invited us to go with her to Wisley and that I doubt not is one of the greatest of them all. Certainly it is from a practical viewpoint even if it can be bettered in spectacle and landscape by less comprehensive gardens. Hidcote, in the

Cotswolds, will remain in my memories as the most beautiful of them all. Its many gardens within a garden keep it to a comprehensible scale; endlessly satisfying, never surfeiting.

Of the smaller gardens which we have enjoyed together, I recall an occasion when on holiday we found a village where, for a single admission charge, in aid of the local Conservation Society, we were offered entry to five gardens. Each was quite perfect and entirely individual, none too large to be assimilated and appreciated to the full. In fact one was not more than forty feet square but contained a camomile lawn, a small rockery and one piece of statuary. Another specialised in roses and one in flowering shrubs. The other two were where my humming-bird came into her own. In the last of these five gardens, tea was being served on the terrace. By then we were among friends, members of the village community who were actively aware of their heritage and watchful for its future.

Being thoroughly British, we are not put off by the weather on these occasions. We travel properly equipped with boots, mackintoshes and umbrellas. Nevertheless we have taken shelter in a remarkable range of buildings: orangeries, summer-houses, gazebos, grottoes and tool-sheds. The most wonderful tool-shed I remember was, and maybe still is, at Horstead House.

The setting of Horstead House, downstream from the site of the former watermill, in an unusual one for that part of Norfolk as we do not often find ground dropping so steeply to the edge of our slow-flowing rivers. A brief climb over mown grass between drifts of flowers and we were able to look back over the house and trees to the flat valley and the village of Coltishall beyond. Through the trees and between large groups of azaleas we could see motor launches and cruisers moving up to the head of navigation at the old lock. On the near side of the island, the water flowed clear and shallow.

Evidence that the waterside beauty of this garden was no accident was to be found in the toolshed. Here we saw dydles and hodders and other long-handled tools to which I could put no names, even one which I swear must have been designed specially for pulling small children out of the river.

A part of the joy of this collection of tools was that it was a working assembly, with scythes and sickles jostling for position alongside motor mowers. Other superannuated items still had their places among newer tools like old men happily retired but still part of the community. There were forks, old and new, for every purpose and I think there must have been a different sort of hoe for every species of weed. Pride of place among the old faithfuls was a bow operated broadcast seeder.

In many respects this toolhouse was the living counterpart of an oil painting which hung for some time on a wall of our bedroom. Painted by Chris Hart and entitled ''The Potting Shed'', the scene took one's eye from a gloomy corner of the shed, past a variety of garden tools and implements, out into the pale light of a garden.

I had a suspicion that the view from the windows of our new home was going to prove rather dull and static after a sea view which was never still for a moment, never lacking in interest and was forever exhibiting its range of moods. It only took a little time to prove how wrong I had been, and I quickly learned to watch and love our new setting in the countryside in all its permutations of change. The main elements in the changing pattern were provided by the seasons themselves, and a complicated interplay with the rotation of crops and weather conditions of the day. Each crop in the cycle offers in turn its own visual pleasures and at times its all-pervading scent.

Perhaps the biggest surprise of all to me was the beauty of the potato crop. As soon as the seed was set and ridged, changes of light and shade meant that at no two times of day did the field look the same. The green tops emerged with almost military precision and soon closed upon each other to form a gently moving deep pile carpet of green. Then came the sudden morning of colour — fluorescent mauve flowers of Maris Peer and the pale blue of earlies on the headlands turned the field into a sea of bloom. A sad moment arrived with the acid spray to kill off the haulm before the harvest, but sadness was soon replaced by the interest and movement of mechanical lifting and harvesting. In a remarkably short time, men, women and machines moved on to their next assignment having delivered the earth of its offspring, leaving only the churned, ridged soil, bleached steams and a few dispossessed representatives of wildlife.

I like to think of somewhere on the farm which is the equivalent of the toolshed where these hugely expensive pieces of equipment rest dustily between their brief periods of seasonal activity. I well understand the compulsions which ever the years have caused farmers to add to their outbuildings, often producing in the process such pleasing groups of buildings. Before we moved home, I was always a short of workshop and outhouse space. I now had what I mistakenly imagined would be a superabundance. There must surely be a variation of Parkinson's Law and a force at work which makes inanimate objects proliferate to occupy all space available in a workship or a toolshed. It is also a notable feature of gardening that houseplants need house-room and blocking up window space is one of their favourite habitats.

I refer, of course, to the inside windowsills. Outside is another province; window boxes are a separate culture with their own literature and traditions.

We had found a new home in which we could live with our houseplants. Double glazing, tiled sills, and central heating all looked propitious. There were faults and deficiencies in other aspects. The kitchen, for one, needed redesigning but this was easily achieved. We chalked out the accommodation area required by the dog and rebuilt the rest of the kitchen around it.

My wife, to whom I will for the moment refer to as 'Greenfingers', accuses me of being insensitive to plants. This is quite unjustified. I have shared a home with plants for some forty years. This has made me understanding, tolerant and, in some areas, very sensitive indeed.

Take Aphelandra for example. I was really sorry for her. She was a transient guest in our home — an exotic and beautiful thing but she was silly and sulky, she couldn't tolerate even the slightest draught. When Greenfingers put her by the open fireplace in summer, she wilted and died before the trouble was identified.

I wish the same would happen to Calpe, the killer cactus. He had his origins in Spain. At about the age of ten (he is now 32), our son went on holiday with friends and brought the infant cactus home among his souvenirs. Like most small creatures, Calpe was soft and quite appealing. He soon hardened off to meet the rigours of the English climate and to seek revenge for the defeat of the Armada. In fact he waxed so exceedingly that eventually we needed to make up a four to lift him out into the sunshine each summer. Calpe today is the fifth generation of that original beast. He lurks vindictively in the hall, hiding behind the Philodendron, waiting to stab the unwary, with all the goading, provactive skills of a true Spanish picador. No-one can be insensitive to Calpe.

They say that a stolen plant always flourishes and I believe the fingers of many a keen gardener are as light as they are green. We have a rambler rose whom we call Alassio. Greenfingers pinched some pieces when we were on holiday. cosseted them in her sponge bag and persuaded them to grow and cover a brick and flint wall in Suffolk. Alassio is sweetly fragrant, full of beauty and nostalgia. We couldn't leave her behind when we moved home. She lived precariously with us in our caravan for six months until re-established in the new garden. This year the gentle blush of her blossom will remind us once again of the Costa Mil Fiori — the sights, scents and sounds of that foreign field, the sad cypresses, fragrant eucalyptus and the soft, waving fronds of palm trees with the sparkle of the Mediterranean beyond. I am not only sensitive to plants, I can even turn quite lyrical.

85

Do you have Culture in your bathroom? We have Culture and Horticulture. Amazing ceramic creations marking various stages in the development of artistic taste and ability of our younger daughter jostle with indoor ivy, voluptuous Tradescantia, pendulous succulents and trailing grasses. Of these, the ivy and grasses are most intrusive. They need to be cut back vigorously before they obscure the taps on the bath or droop their trailing fronds into hot soapy water. I can lie back in the bath and with eyes half closed can see the Green Man peering from the undergrowth, a surrealist ceramic radio sitting silent among the pampas and the neoclassical group in the far corner which transports me to a pine-scented Greek island.

But this Garden of Eden was the scene of the attack on my sensitivities. Being modest by nature, I continued to draw the curtains after the luxuriant growth of plant life had made this a matter of some difficulty. Damage was inevitable. If anyone wishes to peer in through the foliage they can see us in the light which filters in from outside, green like the two children of Woolpit, and being careful not to knock moss, vermiculite or falling leaves into the bath.

Even though a reluctant gardener I can make claim to having produced my fair share of vegetables and I certainly had an active relationship with our chest freezer. A sort of love/hate relationship with very little love. But of course I was concerned when it entered into a terminal decline.

It made laboured, galloping noises which didn't always stop when it was given a good kick. It leaked gently but persistently on the floor. The lid was becoming more and more warped.

As we were about to put our house on the market, it seemed the right moment to make a new start.

First we had to empty it. For two or three weeks we lived rather well. The housekeeping account got into credit but we had to remember to set this against re-stocking at some future date. Then we got down to the mystery bundles at the bottom. I'm easy to feed. Omnivorous you might say, or I have heard the expression 'coarse feeder', but even I was not enthusiastic about a diet of courgettes, Victoria plums (not quite ripe) and purple sprouting broccoli (picked rather past its prime).

We got to the end eventually, disconnected the electricity and sent for the special disposal section of the Local Authority Health Department. This high sounding body turned out to be our old friends the Dustmen, with a bigger than usual vehicle. They opened the rear end and with an easy nonchalance, slung our freezer into the jaws of the machine. It champed and chewed like a monster, ingesting sheet metal, chromium trim and copper pipework.

86

In less than a minute it was all over. The machine came to rest with expanded polystyrene sticking to its teeth and a smell of diesel fumes like mechanical flatulence.

Altogether it was, we felt, a tasteless performance which we would rather not have witnessed. They could perhaps have gone round the corner before dealing so violently with our old servant. At least we thought that it had been our servant.

Eventually we sold our house. From the time we had decided to do so until moving into our new home nearly a year has passed. Almost twelve months of freedom from freezer.

It is strange how labour saving devices, at first hailed as aids to more gracious living, eventually become chores in their own right. There was a time when we sent all our washing to the laundry; the tedious business of listing everything (we averaged 120 articles per week), and stuffing them into a hamper became almost insupportable. The washing machine which followed is a classic example of 'servitor serventium', as they used to say in the N.A.A.F.I. There is no disputing that one works hard to serve washing machines, washing up machines and even carpet cleaners, but it seems to me that the hardest taskmaster of all is a freezer.

As a vegetable gardener, the special deference demanded starts early in the year with the seed catalogue. Only those varieties specially recommended for freezing may be countenanced. It is essential to plan for a surplus otherwise it is likely that one's whole production will have found its way into the chest with never a fresh green pea or string bean being tasted. "Found its way" is an absurd simplification of the work actually involved in harvesting, cleaning, preparing, scalding and packaging these sacrificial items to be presented at the frozen altar. There are also hours of fruit picking to be taken into account and evenings of abstruse mathematical calculations establishing the most economical source of, say, half a lamb, not to mention the time and petrol expended going down to the coast for fresh fish which has quite possibly already made the round trip to Billingsgate and back.

All the time that we were "of no fixed abode", we lived in our caravan on a variety of sites. One of our guiding principles in choice of location has been the season of the year, with special reference to strawberries, raspberries, apples, plums, mushrooms and garden produce. Freedom from gardening was a bonus and the greatest joy of all was eating fresh fruits and vegetables in season, and looking forward to successive crops grown by other people. A sun-warmed strawberry straight from the field is a far greater experience than a thawed out relic at Christmas time. The aroma of tomatoes and the bloom on their skins can never be encapsulated in cold polythene, nor the scent, taste and texture of freshly baked bread as collected from the village baker.

Despite producing daily evidence to the contrary, my wife claims that she is not a good cook. In any case, it doesn't take a genius to wash a lettuce (cut your own, 10p), open a tin of corned beef and pour farm fresh cream on two bowls of strawberries (P.Y.O.). Add some of that fresh bread and I ask for nothing better.

When we were on the way to getting a roof over our heads once more the debate started: To freeze or not to freeze? I only put up token resistance — you can't argue very convincingly when you know that you are wrong.

Even an interest in gardens and horticulture can quickly lead one back to antiques and bygones, as in the case of Euston Hall. We had been there twice in quick succession. The first occassion was to join some friends of ours for a meal before attending a concert in the church. The string quartet was as lively and pleasing as the little seventeenth century building itself, built by Lord Arlington in the Italian style.

We had approached over Knettishall Heath and along the sweeping drive between the trees of Rushford Belts, a mixed woodland of arboreal opulence, Spanish chestnut, beech, oak and many others backed by towering conifers, leading straight into the heart of the thousand acre estate. This is the most spectacular way to come to Euston, to the trim village with its houses set well back from the road which is lined by more trees, each an individual and magnificent specimen.

To arrive from the direction of Elveden is just as beautiful though in a less formal manner. Oak trees meet overhead to form a long green tunnel which at the last encompasses the river as well before one crosses the bridge to enter the park. We came this way on our second visit when the house and park were open to the public in aid of the Red Cross.

I will not dwell long on the house and formal gardens. The former was drastically reduced in size when rebuilt after a fire in 1902 and the latter are not very extensive. Together they form an unostentatious and charming home. What I love is the landscaping of William Kent; the spaciousness of the limewalk to the church, the vista of parkland towards the ''Temple'', the grassed walks of the wooded pleasure garden with its glimpses of small lakes and islands formed by careful control of the amenable little river.

While walking in the garden we fell into conversation with the gardener. It was through him that we learned of the forthcoming sale of furniture to be held at the Hall. The catalogue of the two day sale listed over six hundred lots, a truly amazing collection of items ranging from such as a Victorian water closet with blue and white ceramic liner, a Georgian mahogany measuring wheel and a child's Victorian oval tin bath on detachable stand, to the other end of the scale where there were a Flemish oak two-tiered cabinet, Regency sofas and a monumental carved walnut and pollard oak sideboard.

The auctioneers stated that the reason for sale was that a large number of pieces were formerly among the furnishings of the two wings of the Hall which were burnt down and demolished thirty five years ago. They also stated the obvious fact that this represented something of a 'time capsule' and a rare opportunity for buyers to see such a wide range of items from one source. In fact, we attended Day One only when the action took place in the coach house, brew house and outbuildings.

Bidding was brisk. All the usual faces were to be seen and a great many others as well. It is necessary on these occasions to keep calm and not allow enthusiasm to cloud commercial judgements; an ice-chest or a wash-dolly or an eggrack are still an ice-chest, a wash-dolly or an eggrack even if they did belong to His Grace the Duke of Grafton.

With all the excitement I still managed to slip down to the river. The mown grass was like a carpet beneath my feet. Low-flying jets from Honington screamed overhead but failed to disturb a flock of Canada geese. They, like me, enjoy those last few hundred yards of the Black Bourne before it loses its identity and joins the River Little Ouse.

LOT 8
Sitting Pretty

The last time my wife and I were looking for new fields to conquer we applied for the joint post of custodians at Hughenden Manor. You may be sure that before attending for interview we did a crash course of study and became quite knowledgeable on the subject of Benjamin Disraeli. I confess that little of that hastily crammed knowledge remains with me, beyond a firm impression that our contemporary Prime Ministers are a very dull lot indeed compared with such a colourful character.

We also took note of the local industry around High Wycombe and my interest in what may be called the rural chair received a lasting stimulus. I cannot now remember how much Disraeli paid for those shares in the Suez Canal Company, but I do recall that the output of chairs from High Wycombe reached a staggering peak of five thousand chairs per day in 1870; that eight thousand chairs were supplied to the Crystal Palace and four thousand rushed-seated ones were made for St Paul's Cathedral. As a 'rush-seater' myself that last figure means much to me in terms of toil and broken finger nails and I like to think that the four or five tons of dried rushes probably came from our East Anglian rivers.

Many years earlier, so long ago that it seems like a different life, I went shopping with a friend who wanted to buy a desk for his new office. While he was making his choice I filled in the idle moments by trying out some of the vast range of chairs on offer. Although I had no intention of buying, I found one absolutely right for me and as it was also offered at a special price I bought it and use it still. This chair was covered with thick brown varnish (chipped in places and hence the ''shop soiled'' price). I proceeded to clean it down and to disclose the beautiful grain and colours of elm, beech and ash.

Well chosen wood used in their construction gives me so much pleasure in this style of chair. It took me longer to appreciate the finer points of upholstery work where so much of the skill and craftsmanship is hidden from the eye. Regretfully, in modern furniture much else may also be concealed.

Although relatively modern, mine is directly descended from those traditional Windsor chairs produced around High Wycombe since about 1700. It is this continuity of style which makes these chairs so timeless that one can rarely date them with any confidence. There are exceptions sometimes provided by regional variations such as our own East Anglian Mendlesham chairs which seem to have been produced for a comparatively short period only, around 1830. Their scarcity enhances their value and, not surprisingly, we rate them most highly in East Anglia.

The second chair which has loomed large in my life is a delightful little Victorian; plump and deeply dimpled with buttoning of back and arms. Definitely a lady's chair, it fits me nowhere, but was one of the better presents which I have found for my wife. It served well as a nursing and sewing chair and like all well used articles, eventually showed unmistakable sign of wear. First-aid was administered but in the end it became clear that the patient could be saved only by the full treatment.

Do-it-yourself has long been established as a part of our way of life, which I parallel with a penchant for somewhat offbeat evening classes. So once again I signed on; this time for Upholstery, and entered a strange world of tacks and twine, of wadding, webbing and circular needles.

I am never surprised to observe that people grow to look like their dogs, but I was startled to note that each of the twelve mature students had a definite affinity with the chair on which he or she was working. There was the well stuffed, the angular, fussy, plain and stout, even a rocker who was clearly incapable of immobile repose. Don't think that I am being rude, they were charming, every one of them, and I looked forward each week to the next class where I laboriously stripped and rebuilt that little chair.

It was a social club as well as a class and I think that we all enjoyed the ''twittering sessions'' at the end of each evening when we studied and admired each others' progress. But I think I should warn any potential student that to carry home someone's chair is a very different matter from the more traditional pile of books.

It took me nearly a year to finish my chair and it may be a long time before I tackle another.

My spindle-back grandfather and that deep buttoned Victorian are both very much part of my life but I am haunted by memories of a third chair — the one that got away. It was a memorable chair to sit in. A finely carved rosewood of Regency origins, with cabriole legs, deep buttoned leather upholstery and magnificent brass castors. To say that I sat in it is a terrible understatement. I luxuriated in its comfort. It fitted my every contour; it rested my head and my arms; I could have dreamed in it for hours at a time pretending to read or watching television. At the time it seemed far too much to spend on my own comfort but I know that I shall continue to regret letting the moment pass. If another such paragon should come my way, I will be less parsimonious and would even go back happily to weekly twittering sessions to put it in good order.

Long ago I decided that there must be as many different varieties of chairs as there are people. My experiences at upholstery classes pointed in that direction and encounters with both continue to foster the thought.

We have by now lost tally of the number of chairs with which we had dealings in the Old Forge; they were legion. The ladderback, which was the first on which I attempted rush seating work; the plump little Victorian which I took to upholstery classes; that paragon of a library chair which escaped my clutches; these stand out in my mind as old friends among a host of acquaintances.

Traditional kitchen Windsor chairs are in constant demand. There is a wide appreciation of their individual variations, their fitness of purpose in the strength and relative simplicity of design. We have learned too that when stripped of the almost inevitable coatings of gooey varnish or layers of paint, the beauty of the wood can be a delight. A little hard work with wax polish and a cloth enriches the figuring of their elm seats and the grain of the ash or beech of which the remainder of the chair is usually made. These chairs have climbed the social scale and, teamed with solid pine or elm tables, have found their place in a great many living rooms. We collected them continuously, selling odd singles or pairs and all the time aiming to match up the so desirable sets of four, six or even larger numbers.

Among my prejudices is a great distaste for plywood. I find it impossible to look with pleasure on any piece of furniture which includes this material, even when it has been used for the bottoms of drawers. It is not that lamination is a modern idea (and therefore suspect!). The Thonet factory in Czechoslovakia was turning out bentwood chairs with ply seats as early as 1856 but these give me less pleasure than cane seated ones. A broken cane seat "repaired" by having plywood nailed over it fills me with horror.

One of the first chairs in our stockroom was a gracefully curved Thonet rocker, soon followed by a less elegant but still desirable Victorian spring rocker. This one we had rescued from the Macclesfield canal and restored to working order. A friend of ours once described our occupation as that of "rescuing things and finding homes for them". We liked that better than oblique references to Steptoe & Son though, thinking back to the contents of the house and yard where those two characters lived, it is now clear to me that they were very astute operators.

The earliest known forms of the Windsor come from the mid 18th century. Apart from a few structural developments, there is little about them which fits into a particular period. Like other traditional forms of furniture, these chairs are timeless. The work of the 'bodgers' who produced the turned parts is probably much over remanticised, though I can easily believe that it was a satisfying occupation. They worked right at the source of their raw materials, setting up their ingenous pole lathes

Low-back Windsor chair of Mendlesham type (1830-1850).

in the beechwoods. We hear less of the Bottomers, the men who produced the elm seats. Theirs was a separate, though closely allied, craft. I have never seen one of these shaped seats being produced but I have watched a boat builder of the old school shaping a block of wood for the stern of a boat. He held the block still on the ground with one foot and swung his adze with effortless grace. It seemed that the razor sharp blade was doing all the work under his gentle guidance. He scorned the use of pencil lines and only rarely used a measure. The two crafts clearly had much in common. As factory style of production came in from about 1800, the cottage industry continued for a time alongside the system with the womenfolk working at home, caning and rushing the seats. The mass-produced Windsors of today are still based on the same designs. What they have gained in technical excellence from modern technology they have lost in character and individuality.

It would be tedious to catalogue the many varieties of chairs, or even the Windsor chair alone. Edwin Skull, a manufacturer at High Wycombe in 1866, lists two hundred and two varieties in production at that time. I have a copy of a photograph of a triumphal arch built of chairs. It was, of course, at High Wycombe and had been built to celebrate the visit of the Prince of Wales in 1880. It became the tradition to mark the visits of Royalty in this way and I can think of no more splendid tribute from the people of the town to both the Prince and also to this chair of many virtues.

Though humble in origin and truly prolific, the traditional shapes are also to be found made of woods other than beech and elm; oak, yew, exotic fruit woods, walnut or even willow, but these are the stars seen less often on our provincial stage; aristocrats, perhaps more at ease in richly carpeted showrooms than in the rural setting of our old forge.

It is a feature of life in most rural communities that one is quickly roped in to serve on committees or take part in various fund raising events, so once again I found myself demonstrating the art of rush seating. Not, this time, in aid of the Church Restoration Fund at the Worstead Village Festival, but just up the road at the Church Fete.

I set up my simple equipment in the shade of an old apple tree and started work. The first person to show interest in my activity was a small boy. He watched for some time without saying anyting. At last, he broke the silence with the workds, ''My grandfather can do that and he's blind!'' That cut me down to size.

Other words of wisdom came later in the afternoon from an elderly man who watched me from a distance before coming over and saying, ''You wholly use a lot of spit. I reckon you could use a cup of tea.'' He got one for me, too, but not before he had enlarged on his theme of the efficacy of spit in certain circumstances including, of course, spit and polish and, less likely, the lubrication of nylon bearings in agricultural machinery.

Inevitably someone eventually asked, ''where do you get your rushes?'' I have two answers to this. Imported rushes I buy at great expenses. Local ones I harvest myself.

One of my favourite places for harvesting is not many miles from Willy Lott's cottage, down on the Suffolk border. In some places, the river Stour flows between beds of reeds and rushes. At secluded spots, it is sometimes possible to see pike in the clear, sunlit water; in the late afternoon, a heron may hoist itself from its fishing ground and fly ponderously towards the setting sun while gulls return seawards to the estuary.

You might expect to find plenty of rushes in Norfolk but sadly this is not now the case. Unlike reeds which are still harvested commercially

94

for thatching, hundreds of acres of rush-beds which used to supply the chair makers of High Wycombe, among others, are now defunct. Even Barton Broad, which was a prolific area, now supports only a few isolated groups.

I try to collect sufficient rushes each year for my own use. The only real difficulty is finding them. They have a number of enemies including river pollution, coypu, neglect, and the Anglia Water Authority, so the annual quest becomes increasingly difficult.

So long as the weather is pleasant, a day out getting rushes is a great delight. Wading waist-deep in cool, clear water, cutting and gathering into bundles is not an over-exacting task. I can take it at a gentle pace and enjoy the habitat.

The more regular inhabitants of the stream are often surprised or indignant to meet me. Duck and moorhen retreat swiftly and noisily but when swans appear on the scene I am usually the one to give way rather than argue about riparian rights.

While they are still wet and fleshy, rushes smell quite strongly of fish and mud; a sharp contrast to the delicious scent of hay and aromatic herbs which is characteristic of them some two or three weeks later.

Sunlight dancing on the surface, the gentle pull of the current, the chuckle of water flowing over pebbles or the therapeutic squelch of mud; thoughts of these fill my mind as I work on a rush seat. Twisting, twisting, working the dampened rushes into position, creating something with a clear fitness of purpose has a charm which give me enormous pleasure. The varied greens and browns of the flexible material complement the mellow gold and honey of mature ash and oak, forming a ''rush bottom'' which has not changed in general form for hundreds, maybe thousands, of years.

Another question which I am asked when demonstrating is, ''What started you on this?'' My answer goes back to the time when our younger daughter brought a ladderback chair from Chesterfield to her new home in Norfolk. It needed rebottoming and my wife volunteered to have it done as a housewarming present. The offer was well received but difficult of fulfilment for at that time we could find no-one willing to undertake such work. As time passed and the job remained undone, it began to look like another do-it-yourself situation. I signed on for evening classes (the only male in a class of 28) and from seven till nine each Monday evening was instructed in the intricacies of the ancient craft.

The truth is that there is not really a great deal to learn. Once the basic method has been taught, it then becomes a matter of practice, of developing your own style and learning as you go. Every one of these ancient chairs has some individuality for which the basic rush pattern

The Arch of Chairs at High Wycombe to celebrate the visit of the Prince of Wales in 1880.

has to be adapted.

A footnote to the poster advertising the Church Fete had read, "If wet, in the Village Hall", but the sun shone the whole afternoon so that I was glad of more then one cup of tea and the shade under the old apple tree.

About that time most of my rushwork was going to America. My pleasure had a touch of sadness in it as I watched the results of my labours being loaded up for the first stage of their journey to Kansas City. The honey hue of ash and elm and the mellow green of Norfolk rushes glowed in the sunshine as the chairs were carried into the cavernous interior of the pantechnicon.

Last in was the high ladder-back rocking chair; a beautiful piece of furniture which I was sorry to see go. It had been a pleasure to renew the rushwork and to restore it to a former glory.

There was also a whiff of irony in the situation. "Not quite British" seems to have been history's verdict on rocking chairs, for although it has been, and still is, America's national chair, the rocker has never been entirely accepted as an Englishman's chair.

Benjamin Franklin is sometimes credited with having invented the rocker in about 1760. Perhaps he did, especially if you concede that most inventions are really adaptations of earlier ideas.

It is clear that early example were indeed only adapted ladderbacks; solid wood or rush-botom'd, country-made types of Windsor chairs with curves added. The curves were gentle to offer reasonable stability and kept the rocking sedate.

Not until about 1825 did the first purpose-design emerge. The Boston Rocker appeared as a thoroughbred classic, not to be surpassed and hardly equalled in 200 years. Its seat was deeply curved, with arms to match and slender rods holding a high scroll back to support one's head.

American 'Windsors' were customarily more graceful and lighter than their English counterparts and their legs splayed out somewhat more widely. In spite of having available such delightful woods as hickory and an abundance of fruit-woods, these chairs were more often than not painted. Green was the favourite colour, the more expensive models showing a high standard of decorative painting — mostly scrolls and flowers.

Within 50 years, American rockers were being imported into this country under the name of "Sinclair's American Commonsense Chairs". The ladderback had been replaced by high upholstered or caned backs. They ranged in price from 25 to 35 shillings each.

Meanwhile, on this side of the Atlantic, evolution and innovation had been at work but even by the time of the Great Exhibition in 1851 it is evident that the rocker was not quite socially acceptable. It was offered or excused on medical grounds. The 'Digestive' or invalid chair was recommended for use in the sickroom and of course for nursing mothers and "all ailing members of the weaker sex".

Ten years later, the really innovative use of bentwood rocked the boat. Michael Thonet, the Austrian designer, applied his talents and skills to the production of his splendid Thonet Rocker. The convoluted curves and the length of the chair combined to give elegance and what we might now call 'rockability'. They came with either deep-buttoned upholstery or cane finish. An advertisement in The Graphic of March 31st, 1880, details the upholstered ones thus:

"Stuffed, all hair, 42/-"

"Ebonised and gold ditto, in
velvet and satin, 72/6d"

The Thonet Factory exported considerable numbers to America but they never seriously rivalled the well established Boston.

The next innovation in design came late in the Victorian period from Scotland. This was the 'swing' rocker. It had no 'bends' to rock on the floor and wear out the carpet — a canny touch this — but was on a fixed base which remained stationary. The manufacturers claimed that the chair was: "Silent, smooth and pleasant".

In recent times there have been no real innovations, only attempts to translate old designs in new materials and brave efforts to revive the popularity of bentwood.

I am a traditionalist of deep-seated persuasions and cannot easily be weaned from my preference for a ladderback with a full rush bottom. The worst that I will allow to be said of it is that it is habit forming, an addictive antidote to the hustle and bustle of the world beyond my workshop and my hearthside.

LOT 9
A Broad Canvas

We are probably indebted to Dick Joice for introducing and popularising the word "by-gones". Less tightly defined than antiques, they cover an infinitely wide range of artefacts. One loose definition of a by-gone is that of something which has quite unobtrusively fallen into disuse and is in danger of disappearing. Something like a bell-tent!

Do you remember bell-tents? They seem to me to have belonged to another life; a world of Scouting for Boys, Chums and the British Empire.

I have two splendid photographs of my grandfather, Colonel Hill. In one he is seated on his campaign chair in front of his tent. "Somewhere in Suffolk" is the security conscious caption. One can imagine his surprise if he had been able to see us selling campaign chairs in the Old Forge and his probable indignation about trade in militaria. My grandfather relinquished command of the 1st Volunteer Battalion Norfolk Regiment in June 1907, but was back again with the regiment in the 1914-18 war, defending the Lowestoft area against the threat of invasion. In the second photograph, he is mounted on his charger. The bell tents in the background of the picture are lined up with regimental precision. The Union Jack hangs limply at the flagpole.

Of course, it was possible to make a frightful hash of pitching one of these tents, but if undertaken seriously, it was a relatively simple business to mark out the two concentric circles of pegs, assemble and insert the single pole, raise the whole fabric and adjust the guyropes. There was then, as I recall, a necessity to slacken all guys in anticipation of shrinkage in wet conditions or to roll up and secure the brails to avoid suffocation. On Salisbury Plain, as I also recall vividly, it was always too wet or too hot so that one or other of these measures was always necessary. A third anticipatory action was known as "storm precaution". This entailed encircling the sloping roof of the tent with a rope which was then secured to the ground with additional guyropes.

We slept eight to a tent, each with our feet towards the pole — an adequate allocation of space once the turmoil of getting ourselves "sorted out" had been achieved.

To be honest, there didn't seem to be much more room to spare when, many years later, we took our children camping with one of these veteran tents. We either borrowed or hired it from Mr Lincoln on Pakefield cliff. It was no less venerable than he. We pitched it near the cliff at Mundesley and were lucky that no storm precautions were called for.

I could swear that if led there blindfold I would instantly recognise the inside of a bell tent. I believe that the unforgettable smell was a combination of sweat, mildew, gently decomposing jute, with just a touch of trampled grass, sometimes compounded with socks and army boots. Such is the stuff of which memories are made. Or some of them are, others are less noisesome, like the day I laid aside my apron and all washed and brushed was ready to set off to Norwich for a social engagement.

"Do you know what you are going to say this afternoon?" enquired my wife.

"Yes, I think so," I confessed, rather guiltily, because I had been invited at least three months earlier to present the prizes. I had kept thinking about it from time to time but, as always, when an event is far enough ahead, I had put off serious consideration. Now time had nearly run out.

"I suppose," I said, "that there are three things to be mentioned. First to offer my thanks for the honour of being invited for this rather special 50th Anniversary occasion. Second, to say something about the achievements of those fifty years, and then to round off with something amusing or even faintly memorable."

"Well, try not to be a bore and don't go on too long," advised my wife. As she is an ex-schoolmistress and we have been married for forty years, she does know what she is talking about.

The afternoon was warm. The marquees stood taut and beautifully pitched on the immaculate lawn. My mind wandered over fifty years and became channelled on all those family occasions where the action had taken place in marquees.

The earliest of these was some years ago whem my wife and I attended a sale of the contents of the house which was to become our first home. I realize now that it was a humdrum little sale, not even qualifying for that much overworked adjective, 'important'. For us it was an event of great drama and excitement. The lots which we bought were carried back into the house to become the nucleus of our own furnishings. My wife reliably informs me that of those items only our oak bed and a heavy aluminium frying pan survive.

It was a happy home and a good place to bring up children. The next time a marquee was erected in the garden was for the wedding of our elder daughter. In the intervening years, we had attended a variety of events bounded by canvas walls — speech days, prize-givings, flower shows, gatherings of all degrees of formality at Oxford and Cambridge.

If the wedding of our elder daughter had been a fairly formal occasion, that of our younger was definitely not. Right from the beginning we were aware of other forces at work. A determination for nonconformity struggled with an inherent respect for the traditional tribal rites. Even the marquee fitted into the happy pattern of informality. It was not so much a marquee as two ends which were laced together to form a circle like a miniature circus tent. There was even a do-it-yourself element about it as all hands were pressed into service to get it erected in half a gale of wind.

None of these events had we enjoyed more than periodic school reunions in Norwich, where the sight of a gleaming marquee with a background of clipped yews and beech trees is one which fills me with pleasure. It is a pleasure enormously enhanced when I see it set in this scene of my childhood and peopled by my oldest friends.

I was roused from my reverie by the mention of my name. Then I was on my feet, presenting silver cups and prizes to a succession of small boys. As their names were called, they came up to the table, uncomfortably clean and tidy and with varying degrees of eagerness or self consciousness. It was almost impossible to believe that fifty years ago I had been one of those to come up and collect a cup. Impossible but true, for I was one of the founder pupils. The Headmaster was just saying as much.

Nemesis arrived.

There was a time, my friends may tell you, when I was prepared to get on my feet and make a speech at the drop of a hat. Not so now. I am happily out of practice. I tried to remember what I had said to my wife and to act on it.

Inevitably I reached a point where I had predicted that I would be floundering for a finish. I floundered. Then I told of a 50 year old memory of my father.

The occasion had been the time when, like a member of my audience, I had come to the end of my prep school days and was about to go way to public school. My father, like any good Norfolk man, was economical in the use of words. He didn't make a big production of it. What he said was: "Well, old son, good luck! You will meet all sorts of people; never do anything you'd be ashamed to tell me about."

Everyone was very charming to me. I thoroughly enjoyed the rest of the afternoon. I hope that I didn't go on too long and that I wasn't too much of a bore.

Auction sales in marquees are comparatively rare events these days. They have an atmosphere all of their own which has nothing to do with socks and army boots though certainly damp canvas and crushed grass are noticeable features.

One such my wife and I attended on the outskirts of the village of Needham. An idyllic place really in which it was quite a shock to find two fields turned into temporary car parks with fluorescent jacketed policeman on duty and a crowd far exceeding the whole population of the parish.

The Auctioneer's catalogue stated that the sale would be signposted for viewing and on Sale Day the ample carparking arrangements to the west of the house would be clearly indicated, but that care was essential on this busy road. I love auctioneers' catalogues. They are documents of such sunny optimism and hopeful promise with any clouds of doubt tucked away as conditions and special conditions of sale in the small print on the back pages.

The day had improved as my wife and I drove along the Waveney Valley and as we reached the village the last of the mist dispersed in warm sunshine. I would have liked to visit the little medieval church which has a typical round flint tower with a less typical octagonal addition but the business of the day was pressing. Nor was there time that day for a side trip to "Sparrows Mill" on the Suffolk side of the river.

But there were some moments for contemplation towards the end of the day. All the lots in the meadow and the marquee had been sold. The Auctioneer had moved into the house to sell carpets and curtains which interested me not at all. The aftermath of the day's activities lay scattered as people claimed their purchases like looters in a pillaged town.

As I stood there the flapping of canvas brought me back to the garden in Needham. The once so neatly pitched marquee was in disarray, the captains and the kings were all departing. I was left with my thoughts and I know that I will always enter a marquee with a sense of occasion; with feelings compounded of happy memories and pleasurable anticipation.

As I stood there I thought all over again about marquees and our daughters' weddings. Even though the two of them were married within quite a short space of time, we had inevitably moved home. Nevertheless I had thought that it would all be quite straightforward and easy. You see, in addition to many other qualities of excellence, my wife is methodical. She had a well filled manilla folder marked "R's wedding"; all the details of that first occasion were in there, including the final addition of a sheet headed "Lessons learnt".

Of course it was clear that there would be differences. The first time we didn't have a house to live in. The whole of the advance organisation and planning took place in a small caravan out in the heather in North Norfolk. Our daughter was teaching in Sicily and her fiance was in Oxford. There were times when the caravan seemed more like Montgomery's H.Q. than a temporary home.

But it all worked out splendidly on the day: the sun shone, the cameras clicked, the church was beautiful and so was the bride. In fact it all went according to the book, as they say, but don't ask me which book as there seems to be an endless supply of literature on the subject of weddings.

So with this sort of precedent, with a house to live in this time, and everyone concerned within a reasonable distance, I thought that it would be easy. What I hadn't allowed for a difference in personalities involved. Our first daughter was willing and eager to "go by the book"; our second was not.

Right from the beginning we were made aware of other forces at work, and a pattern began to emerge. It was an interesting compromise between established tradition and a desire to be different: a wish for non-conformity struggling with an inherent respect for the tribal rites.

For starters, they had not been "Engaged", they were just "going to be married", and we were not allowed to use the word Fiance. The design and printing of the wedding invitations gave warning to everyone that this was no run of the mill occasion, and the result was a pleasing example of graphic design with a nice feel for colour. The style was repeated in the printed Order of Service sheets.

By this time I too had begun to question the Establishment, as you might say, and by the time I had been told that I had no need to make arrangements for a morning-dress suit, I really understood that things were going to be different. Even the Vicar seemed to aid and abet this mood of change. "It's your wedding", he said to our daughter, "you tell me how you would like things done." So of course she did.

He was a charming chap, that vicar. Only a couple of months earlier he had invited me to go along and see the bellringers in action. Except for the fact that I would never have wished to offend him, I can't think why I accepted the invitation. I had always found campanology a subject easy to resist. Yet, looking back to childhood, I can recall the fascination of those bellropes in the village church. They ran up and up to disappear through well worn holes in the pine boards which seemed to be about halfway up the tower.

I believe that in childhood, as in old age, we have a greater appreciation of routine. There is a comfort in having an established order and in taking part in well-known ritual. Sunday Mattins always always followed its appointed course. There was never any difficulty about old or new versions. The end of the service, perhaps because it was over-eagerly awaited during the sermon, was as predictable as a homecoming from a long journey.

The sights and sounds were all familiar; the Blessing, a short pause and the creak of bellows before the organ burst forth for the recessional. Then choir and vicar were all in the vestry. Another moment of silence preceded the final prayer, immediately followed by the crash of brass curtain rings as the black curtains were dashed across, screening the vestry from the congregation.

Then it was permissible to gather together one's personal belongings ready for the imminent release out into the shade of the limewalk and thence up the hill and home for lunch. It was during those few moments of leaving the church that it was possible to gaze at the bell ropes which drew the eye upwards but disclosed so little.

So it may have been an unconscious need that caused me to accept the invitation and present myself at nine o'clock, prompt, on New Year's Eve.

It was not at the little flint and thatch building of those early days but at one of the mighty, impressive wool churches of which we boast in East Anglia.

I was taken up to a spacious chamber, well lit, with whitened walls and a floor of wide oak boards. The only splash of colour was provided by the ''pulls'' on the eight ropes which hung in a large circle.

The ringers were assembling. I had a half-formed opinion that bellringers were a rather beery lot of old reprobates with much in common with the less reputable of rugger clubs. If this assembly was typical, then I had been very wrong. The average age must have been less than thirty. The oldest of the party was the vicar himself, who was the first to remove his coat and take hold of a rope. He was joined by the others and they were soon absorbed in the mysteries of a touch of ''Grandsire Triples.''

I was told that the bells were half-muffled. A carpetlike pad on one side of the clappers had the effect that at every other pull the full sound of the peal was followed by a sort of subdued echo. I had previously heard it only in the distance. It was a weird and mournful sound, entirely appropriate for a dirge over the dying year.

As the various changes were rung out, each followed by the dull muffled echo, it was not too fanciful to think that the old year lay a-dying and that we were the mourners. The ringers were clearly too absorbed in their work to think of anything else. Change ringing requires very close attention. One false move and the whole ''touch'' falls apart to become a formless jangle.

After a while they came to an end. The comfortable silence was soon filled with chatter. The ringers changed places. The vicar relinquished the rope of the huge tenor bell and it was clear to see why he had removed his coat before starting his strenuous stint.

At about ten-thirty we adjourned to the vicarage for sandwiches, hot mincepies and coffee. It was a welcome break for all and a warming one for those of us who had not been energetically employed.

After supper, handbells were produced. The ringers stood in a semi-circle and tried their hands at some touches of "Triples" and "Caters". At eleven thirty we all returned to the tower.

One last farewell to the old years was rung and then "Lofty" was sent up the ladder to remove the muffles from the clappers.

And then it was midnight.

The vicar, now back on the tenor, gave twelve pulls to strike the hour. At the last pull, the treble man led off and the whole peal crashed out in a joyful welcome to the newborn year.

About this time I recalled that following R's wedding a number of guests had said what a happy day it had been and how much they had enjoyed the informality. I had thought it to have been one of the most formal days of my life, so I began to wonder with interest rather than apprehension what reactions might be expected.

Of all that goes to make ready for a wedding, the role played by the bride's father is undoubtedly the least obtrusive. It is more in the nature of a spectator with a cheque book. But my brief spell of action came at last. Suddenly the house was quiet; everyone else had gone to the church and there I was alone with my daughter. When were we last alone together? I could only think of a time when we had been sailing — both of us had been a little frightened by the boisterousness of the wind and waves; both of us were enjoying the sensation, perfectly happy and confident in each other's company. This was how we were again; very happy but in need of a little mutual support to go forward. She was a beautiful and slightly tremulous bride, and I was a proud and somewhat nervous father — this much at least was entirely traditional.

I feel sure that we must have chatted foolishly about nothing in particular as we waited for the car to take us to the church. My thoughts were like a replay of a record I had heard before, "Here I go again, handing over a daughter to a young man I don't know very well" and it crossed my mind that whatever their shortcomings, arranged marriages must have been a great comfort to the parents.

We were ready far too soon, and time stood still. At ten minutes to one I went and washed by hands very slowly — I dried them slowly and looked in the mirror for a long time. I came out on the landing and it was still ten minutes to one.

Together we went down the stairs and made getting into the car last as long as we could. Even then we were too early, but we couldn't just sit there so the driver set off and drove at such a funereal pace that we got the giggles. The sound of the bells helped us back to reality.

The village church is like a young cathedral. The ladies of the Flower Club had certainly spread themselves and answered the challenge of a setting almost daunting in size. It was very beautiful. We made our entry to Bach's Suite No. 3 in D Major. With the possible exception of the choice of "Fight the good fight" for the second hymn, the service went along happily and unexceptionally to the Processional.

— Trumpet Voluntary, Clarke —

This was a big moment, for the organist was joined by a trumpet player. The music carried us all back up the aisle at break-neck speed, and that glorious sound rolled round the vast church like a tea clipper roaring home on the Trade Winds.

There was nothing formal like a Reception Line; indeed there was nothing very formal about the marquee itself. Being a circular affair the whole effect was rather as if the circus had arrived.

I think that's just about the point where one could draw a veil (not that there had been one in evidence) or at least resort to a row of asterisks. The corks popped and the bride's father, no longer needed, was allowed to drift off into a happy alcoholic haze.

LOT 10
Suffolk Beetles

One of winter's gales brought down an elm tree which feel across the brook and blocked the footpath. It was not a giant, even compared with that recorded by Gilbert White in 1703 at Selborne in similar circumstances. Nor was it an excess of public spiritedness which caused us to clear the debris.

The lop and top provided many cheerful fires to sit round and the more serious lumber we stacked ready for sawing.

It had been a pollarded elm, one of several surviving in the area which had evidently provided fuel and building material for cottagers of earlier times. As nothing had been cut from it for many years, the top growth was heavy and proved too much for the hollow trunk so that it was doomed even before Dutch elm disease got hold of it.

Now that elms have almost disappeared from the hedgerows of our landscape it is, I am sure, only a matter of time before scarcity makes it much more sought after.

It is not only good burning properties that makes elm desirable. Pollarded specimens produce beautifully convoluted patterns of grain. Strikingly evident when used for the seats of Windsor chairs, they complement the straight grain of pine or marry happily with a well selected elm table. "Poor man's oak", it is sometimes called, and as such I am entitled to enjoy its beauty to the full.

Even the jagged stump of that old tree had a strange statuesque quality. Beneath the loose bark were a series of engravings, the work of Bark Beetles, like mysterious writings of an unknown civilization. Sadly the only possible translation of these hieroglyphics is the death sentence for elms.

The removal of the stump took skilful work with a J.C.B. by men from the river authority — men who tend our little brook and keep if flowing sweetly through the valley. I watched them and admired the competence with which they handled the machine.

I am always happy to watch a good craftsman and am frequently delighted by the beauty to be found in so many tools and articles of utilitarian origin. Many of these passed through our hands at the Old

Forge. From awls and augers through bill hooks and mattocks to Suffolk bettles, the list seems endless and it was not always easy to part with them. I am happy to have had good and sufficient reason for keeping the best of the woodworking tools.

The same gale which brought down the elm took the top clean out of a greengage tree in our garden. Being a cottage garden of long standing we had a good collection of fruit trees. Most of them well past their prime and exhibiting excusable eccentricities of age. Gnarled and twisted as with arthritis; some leaned and shrank from the prevailing wind; all blossomed and fruited in a somewhat erratic manner.

We planted new varieties; efficient little half-standards which bear fruit disproportionate to their size. It will be many years before they achieve the mellow mossy beauty of their elders.

My wife and I debated the future of the headless trunk of the greengage. I had a scheme to cut and season its timber for use in the workshop. The notion of future generations being puzzled by and probably unable to identify the wood gave me pleasure. It is doubtful if the quality of the wood would have been sufficiently high for use in furniture, so an easy alternative would have been the log pile and some fragrant fires on the open hearth.

My wife's plan was to leave the decapitated trunk standing and allow it to be host to a Clematis Montana Rubens so we collected one from the garden centre and started it on its nine feet climb to splendour.

What we had both forgotten was that the old tree had also been host to successive generations of flycatchers. In the spring they were back again. Quite undisturbed by the tree having lost all its branches, they built their nest in the well worn hollow only five feet from the ground. By June the parents were busy feeding their young. I would like to be able to record, as did Gilbert White, ''... a garden perfumed with roses and a lawn with a net across it for lawn tennis or set with croquet hoops and a little bird darting from the net top to make short circular fly-fishing tours of the air.'' Sadly, we did not live quite so graciously. Our flycatchers operated from the top of the wire netting which kept our geese out of the vegetable garden, while the geese themselves grazed the grass on which no croquet ball could possibly run true.

My sister reminded me recently that one of our grandmothers played croquet for the county. I had quite forgotten that but was able to remind her of another story from our childhood.

''Those men tossing the hay make a delightful scene'', a remark, needless to say, remembered from childhood, for where but in the scenes of our youth can we see men tossing the hay? The words were spoken by the late Gordon Dodson as he sat painting in the water meadow just about Cringleford bridge. My sister and I had climbed the low stone wall which runs up to the bridge and had scrambled down the grassy slope to watch him at work. It mattered nothing to us that he was probably less well known as a painter of the Norfolk scene than his wife Mary, who, incidentally, continued to use her maiden name, Lyle. About that same time, it must have been no later than 1927, Eaton Hill was the biggest thing in my small experience. From beyond the end of the tramlines the road seemed to drop down through a gorge with impenetrable woods growing on either side — it went on down and down till at last it emerged into the sunlight and the village. I can still recall the sense of outrage which I experienced when contractors arrived and tore the hillside apart. The trees were felled and a narrow gauge railway track laid to trolley away the tons of sand and chalk to the lorry loading point somewhere in front of the Cellar House. Eventually the new roadway was built, grass sown and new trees planted. Time healed the scar.

Then, years later, it all happened again. Houses were destroyed, trees felled, gardens sliced away and more tons of soil and chalk displaced. With the mechanical diggers and graders went the scenes of other early memories. Once, when returning home from the village, I ran away from a guardian nursemaid. To delay pursuit I threw may cap in a gateway, relying on her good sense of values to stop and look for it. My ruse succeeded, but the gateway has now too disappeared. Almost as surely it was the same one at which I was later bitten by an alsatian while I was delivering parish magazines; a most unjust circumstance which still rankles.

The Cringleford bypass cuts a swathe right through the playground of our early days. We knew the river Yare all the way up to Colney. It was a playground of enchantment where we spent many summer hours learning to swim and 'messing about in boats'. We knew it in all moods and seasons, in times of ice and flood as well as when the swans were nesting and the water meadows were bright with Kingcups. We used to paddle our flat bottomed boat up as far as the shallow waters below Earlham bridge. We had many a picnic along its banks in the eternally sunny summers of remembered youth. I am assured that at quite an early age I even took my future wife along that enchanted water-way, but the river was then my only love so I was lucky to meet her again several years later.

Our excursions downstream were less frequent, but we knew the shallows behind Eaton church, and the deep pit with the clear chalk bottom where the streams from Keswick and Cantley Run join at a bend of the river. We knew the still beautiful Keswick mill and on occasions

109

made the full passage to Trowse, but the more intimate waters above Cringleford were the true centre of my universe.

Seen from water level the bridge is a fine sight with its double arch and the massive central pile cutting the water like the bow of a salt caked coaster. The stone-capped causey slopes gently up from the Cringleford side while the embanked roadway runs high above flood level to the Red Lion, the village and the twice shattered hill of my memories.

The swift current through the arches is lost below the bridge in the almost still dark water of the pit, some fourteen feet deep; so different from the tree shaded stream above. Here foaming water from the weir beside the millhouse joins the flow round the island from the old wooden sluice. My memories of this place are like watered silk, shot through with sunshine and the flash of kingfisher.

Many years later I wrote about that small incident and was delighted to receive a letter form the vicar of Cringleford. ''The painting to which you refer'', he wrote, ''is hanging no more than a few yards from the spot where you watched it being created ...'' I accepted his invitation to go and see it above a fireplace in the vicarage. The painting was not exactly as I remembered it all those years but Cringleford bridge itself, seen from the meadows or even from the new bypass, still stands strong and beautiful.

Many of the objects we handled in the old forge recalled other scenes and events of my childhood. None more strongly than the big pine kitchen dresser.

My mother's household management and accounts were centred on a pine dresser in our kitchen which housed a number of tins. The most exciting of these was the Egg Tin. This was the one which boasted a trading account. All the others received their periodic doles which were disbursed to their predetermined recipients such as Milkman and Grocer.

The Egg Tin could more properly have been called the Poultry Account; pullets and feed stuffs were bought; eggs and an occasional boiling fowl were sold. I don't know if the tin benefited when we ate one of our own hens, but I believe that cash was transferred from the Grocer's Tin for eggs consumed by the household. What I do know for certain is that somehow the account managed to show a profit and it became a family tradition for mother to raid it to take us all to the Pantomime soon after Christmas.

Another well remembered feature of that dresser is the coffee grinder which was screwed on the left-hand end. Coffee never smelled so good as when I was allowed to climb on Cook's chair, pour some roasted beans into the brass bell-mouth and grind them by turning the handle. When they had all disappeared into the machine, the metal drawer at the bottom could be pulled out by its brass knob and there was the beautiful brown fragrant pile of ground coffee. Oddly enough, it was a good many years before I enjoyed drinking the stuff but the keen pleasure of grinding it has never dulled.

Above the pine dresser was a row of bells, each mounted on its coil spring and operated by a system of wires from the "pulls" in various parts of the house. The Tradesman's Entrance was the one most frequently heard. Nearly everything was brought to the house including two milk deliveries each day. It was understood that the early delivery was from the overnight milking but the midday milk was fresh.

The Milkman's name was George. He was a good friend of mine. When I went to school, about half a mile along the road, I was taken on the 'step' of my father's bicycle and came home at lunch time on the milk cart. I believe that to carry a passenger on the step of a bicycle is now illegal. It was a useful addition to a bike and I was always intrigued by the manner in which many elderly men used it for mounting instead of swinging a leg over in the more usual manner.

George would turn the cart at our gateway and replenish his small delivery can from a large churn on the cart. Inside this can hung pint and half pint measures which he dipped and poured into our jugs. The horse nibbled contentedly at the grass verge.

A second wall in that kitchen was largely occupied by a black cooking range. I don't remember it being used as it had been superseded by a gas cooker and an Ideal boiler for heating water. My mother had learned her household management at an early age and had shouldered much of the responsibility when her mother had become confined to a wheelchair. From tales which she told me, running the household of a country doctor was no small undertaking. Her descriptions tallied so closely with "Mrs Beeton's Household Management" that the one could easily have been the model for the other. In that kitchen the cooking range would most certainly have been black leaded until it shone and the steelwork rubbed with emery cloth to the brightness of silver.

We had a deep sink in the big kitchen. It was used for flower arranging during the week and for laundry on Mondays. Beyond the kitchen was the scullery which had a copper wash boiler in one corner. This was the heart of Monday's washday operations. The fire beneath was lit early and water for it carried in from the pump in the yard. The pump drew not from a well but from an underground cistern which collected rainwater from the roof. Soft water was superior to hard tap water for laundry purposes until Hudsons Primrose Soap was replaced by synthetic detergents.

The pump in the yard was identical to the many we sold in the old forge. The trademark of a rampant horse was certainly the same and so too the unforgettable rasp and clank as the handle is 'pumped'. Inevitably they need priming, with a jug of water poured into the slot at the top before they will deliver.

Mine was a happy childhood, lived out among a comfortable and well ordered household. Comfortable, I believe, because it was well ordered and certainly not because there was an abundance of cash about. At this distance, I see those days as an interesting transitional period in the inexorable social revolution. We still had living-in domestic help, though a very attenuated staff compared with my mother's earlier days before the first world war. I see them too as a time of relative stability. There were still 78 countries in the family of the British Empire and the Scout's Promise epitomised my beliefs and loyalties. It still does.

Working in our workshop or in the old forge among these survivors from the past it was impossible not to look back with nostalgia to childhood or to speculate about earlier times. Perhaps none was more evocative than a beautiful pub settle which we bought. It is sometimes possible to trace the origins and history of a piece of furniture. Not so in this case, my efforts foundered in a London saleroom where romance fell victim to sordid commerce. We were obliged to fall back on our own imaginations.

The elm tree from which it had been made was undoubtedly growing before the discovery of America. As we loaded the settle onto the truck, I was very conscious of the time scale and also of the remarkable contrast between the venerable piece of furniture and the glossy example of twentieth century transportation.

Among the many features we had noted during the period of restoration in our workshop had been two wrought iron handles strategically placed low down at the rear. Even with these cleverly placed handles William and I could only just move it. We wondered how often it had been moved. Clearly it was not thought of as a readily portable piece of furniture and nor was this the general case.

Strictly a country style piece of furniture, settles, in their early 16th and 17th century form, were more readily found in inns and taverns of the countryside than in gracious drawing rooms. High backed settles developed as draught-free refuges, often as an extension of the inglenook. Like other contemporary items of tavern furniture, they were required to be hardwearing and well able to stand up to constant use.

High backed and full skirted, this particular one was eight feet long. Yet despite its size and weight, the gentle curve of its crescent shape and the well contrived slope of the back invited occupation and gave comfort in return. The single slab which formed the seat had been cut from carefully selected timber so that the grain followed the curve. The end piece had been cut from straight grained elm and shaped to form rudimentary wings and armrests. We never did identify the wood from which the panelled back had been made but told ourselves vaguely that it was fruit wood.

Many settles, especially those of a later date, and ones which were built into permanent positions, have boxed in space below the seat to give storage room and sections of the seat hinged for access. The back, too, sometimes became a cupboard, often known as a bacon cupboard. It is clear from some old illustrations that the space below, when left open, could be occupied by sleeping dogs or even a sitting hen with an eye for comfort.

It is evident that such settles were multi-purpose pieces which evolved and developed into day beds, elaborately carved low-back settles and were eventually emasculated and transformed into upholstered settees. Such developments ousted the settle from the domestic scene but it has lingered on in ancient inns from Cornwall to the Highlands of Scotland.

When we had finished our work of cleaning and repair, we started working with wax polish. We were soon rewarded by the way the wood responded, glowing and revealing its nature; the smooth close texture of fruit wood and the delightful graining of elm. There were blemishes, too, mute witnesses of use and misuse, scars carried by a venerable survivor of the centuries.

Eventually we could do no more and moved the settle into the old forge. The space at one end of the thatched building was never part of the smithy and had been divided off by a partition wall of wattle and daub. In this section there was an ancient faggot oven for baking bread, large handwrought iron hooks on the oak beams and a toil-worn floor of gentle undulations. Here we set the scene with some care and a good deal of enjoyment. We found a suitable table on which to place some tankards and a shove half-penny board, a pair of sporting prints to decorate the white walls, and an armful of logs for the corner by the oven. It was very snug. William hung an old ash walking stick on one arm of the settle and said, "Arthur's just gone out, he'll be back in a minute." The scene was set.

Or, if you are a cynic, you might say that the cheese was in position and the trap was set. We didn't have to wait long for our favourite mouse. Not that you would recognise our friend from such a description. A southern belle from Nancy Astor country, she not only recognised a good piece of country furniture but wasted no time making up her mind.

"I've got to have that," she said as she walked in and saw the settle.

113

We invited her to sit on it and have a long cool drink while she thought aloud of her bank balance and what her husband Max would say.

All of which explains how it came about that the next day we were loading yet another piece of our heritage, saved from destruction, for despatch in the wake of the Pilgrim Fathers.

Last Christmas we had a letter from Max and Celeste in their new home in Texas. They enclosed a photograph of the living-room. The sun streams in on the old settle and a rushseated chair against the white plastered wall has a familiar look about it.

LOT 11
Full Cycle

It happened that circumstances so transpired that I found myself in the long unaccustomed stated of having no car in which to go to work. Well, it was only about four miles from home, too far perhaps to contemplate walking, but surely no great distance on a bicycle?

Luckily William was not at home or he might have reminded me of stories of how I used to cycle home for the weekend from Colchester, a matter of sixty miles, in four hours. On that basis I need allow myself only twelve minutes for my short journey to work. It seemed prudent to allow twenty.

Unluckily, William also had his bicycle with him together with the pump from the rather small machine which my wife sometimes rides, so a large slice of my twenty minutes was taken finding a neighbour with a bicycle pump. One hundred strokes each for front and back tyre meant that I didn't even start the ride fresh.

Already I could hear echoes of a remark my neighbour passed about another enterprise in which I nearly failed. "The trouble is", he said on that occasion, "you aren't really up to it!"

But away I went ignoring the absence of cross-bar and swinging my leg round in the proper male fashion. I nearly fell straight off as the saddle was several inches lower than I expected. After that the rhythm of it all came back to me like a well remembered poem and I soon felt the exhilaration of cool fresh air and the morning sun.

As I rode through Redgrave it occurred to me that you might think it to be a rather has-been place. There is Hall Lane but no hall, Mill Lane but no mill, there is Half Moon Lane but the Half Moon last heard the call of "Time, gentlemen, please" over a quarter of a century ago. It was reportedly a friendly little inn. Probably alehouse is the better word as that was the extent of its licence and there was no accommodation for travellers.

Today it is just one of an attractive row of houses and cottages along the edge of what was once the village green. It is thatched, low ceilinged and snug. The bakehouse and ovens which were associated with it have long since disappeared but wild hops grow in profussion among the surrounding hedgerows. The common factor of yeast often brought together the activities of baking and brewing, when both of these were local products with characters as individual at the inhabitants themselves.

Mrs Banham, widow of the last landlord, told me that she never saw those ovens but that when first married she used a 'bush' oven. They were hard work, she says, but properly used produced wonderful results. Faggots were fed into the oven itself and a brisk fire kept going until the bricks turned white. Then all the hot ash was pulled out onto the floor and after a quick sweep round the prepared items were placed inside; bread first at the back, tarts and other small items needing less time at the front.

We had just such an oven at the back of our old forge. A number of customers admired it and some even suggested that they would show us how to use it. They never did but it made a good focal point for displaying such items as dough bins, proving cupboards and other breadmaking and kitchen equipment.

When Dutch ovens were introduced, built so that the fire heated the oven from outside, baking, and particularly clearing up afterwards, became a less laborious business. Like all newfangled ideas, they were regarded with suspicion. My suspicion is that for all her eighty years, Mrs Banham still thought of her "real" bush oven with affection and a nostalgic twitch of her nose for the small of baking or roasting which had filled her cottage every two or three days.

A clue to the second name from the past is provided by the heraldic beast which surmounts the village sign standing on the Knoll. Nicholas Bacon, from whose arms this derives, was the son of a Suffolk yeoman farmer and an outstanding graduate of Corpus Christi, Cambridge.

His first wife, Jane, although a frail creature, bore him three sons and three daughters. The building of their mansion at Redgrave was still proceeding when Anne Cooke, second daughter of Anthony Cooke, appeared on the scene as a helper and companion to Jane. It is understandable that Jane was happy enough to share her responsibilities for the upbringing of her children and the management of the considerable household. She did know that she was handing over to someone who would eventually succeed her and take her place as wife and stepmother.

Anne Cooke saw the completion of Redgrave Hall. It was built on the site of a monastic hunting lodge. Its spacious rooms included 20 for the use of the family and a like number for their servants. There were kitchens, pantry, bakehouse, stillroom and a great range of outbuildings including organgery and fishponds, all surrounded by a deer park. From the only illustration that I have seen, I judge it to have been fairly typical Tudor mansion, built around a central concourse, with decorative twisted chimneys, corbelled stone windows and castellated heads, a splendid country seat, sadly demolished in 1960.

The last triadic ghost, the mill, has been the most difficult to run to earth. My enquiries around the village produced what seemed like conflicting evidence. However, it eventually became clear that there had been a plurality of mils in the area. Not only that, but that at least one postmill had been taken down and re-erected on another site. This mill had the fairly unusual feature of a cartwheel fitted at the end of the tailpole to ease the heavy work of pushing the mill round to face the wind.

It was demolished by fire in 1023; the cause of the fire is unsure. When oe is relying on what might be called 'the oral tradition', the truth is sometimes clouded. It is often necessary to make inspired paraphrasing of such information as "that must have been afore my grandfather's time" or "quite some time before Mother's sister got married".

In our homes and in our cars we have insulated ourselves from our environment. Swinging along on a bicycle I met it once more full in the face and welcomed it with all my senses. That short distance which I have traversed countless times became as full of significance as if seen for the very first time.

From the eminence of my sedate progress I saw over and through hedges which are more usually the limits of my vision as I flash by. It became clear to me why water so often covers the road at one point; a pond lies behind the hedge; it evidently feeds the ditch and all three are of much the same level. Further on a second pond revealed itself as a miniature water garden; an enclave at the bottom corner of the orchards with an ecology of its own; a whole range of waterlife existing so unexpectedly close to the road. It had remained unseen by me as at that point my eyes are invariably on the sharp bend which lies ahead.

Children arriving at the village school unleashed more memories. In particular that same scene in the cold grey light of early morning on election day. Two of us standing stamping our feet. Waiting for the voters. It would have been an overstatement to have said that election fever gripped the village.

"Good morning, madam. Would you care to tell me your number?"

"How would you like Whitehall 1212?"

"I expect that I shall be a little tired of that sort of joke by the end of the day."

But, as things turned out, not too many people were facetious and very few indeed declined a polite invitation to disclose their electoral roll number.

Presently the Presiding Officer left the comfort of his bright warm schoolroom to come out and see how we were getting on. I had started the day well by formally seeking his permission to act as a teller outside his polling station. He had responded handsomely by unlocking another door of the school so that we would be able to take shelter if the weather turned sour.

Previous experience had also taught me that one's brief existence as a teller can be greatly ameliorated if a happy relationship is quickly established with any other tellers on the job. On this occasion, one ''opposition'' teller arrived late and the other party never turned up at all. I trade the ten or so numbers I had collected for information, and thereafter we worked happily together to mutual advantage.

The village slowly came to life around us. A few people on their way to work stopped, climbed from their cars, tractors or motorbikes and strolled over.

''Morning, Jack. In here as usual?''

''No, not that way, old mate; they're in the other room this time.''

''He thinks he's back at school again and he never could read, not even then.''

''Hellow, David, you're about early. My wife will be along later, or she should be, I gave firm instructions.''

''You two have got a cold job here this morning. You ought to change about with them inside — my word, that's something warm in there. No wonder the kids catch everthing that's going.''

''When I came to school here that poind was much bigger. When it froze, we used to slide right across to the road.''

'''Morning, Dan! Thought I'd better come and do my duty early.''

''No, sorry, I can't remember my number.''

''They will tell you inside.''

''All right, I'll give it to you on the way out.''

Between the two of us we knew most of the people coming in at that time of day. Later we were relieved by our wives, and from all accounts they found themselves in much the same position as housewives and busy mothers found time to come and vote on their way to the shop.

By 6 o'clock in the evening I was back at the school again — a different situation by this time of day, with a fairly steady stream of arrivals and departures and less time for sociability, it was more of a scramble to get all numbers recorded. I did remember to go inside and vote!

The scene was familiar. In our rural constituency, political activities such as public meetings and the culminating act of voting for forever inextricably associated in my mind with children's paintings pinned up on the walls, with rows of chairs too small for adult comfort, a few jam-jars full of wild flowers and a permeating smell of polish and gymshoes.

I remembered the first time my wife and I had attended a Parish Meeting in that same room. It was so prefect that we feared to attend another lest the magic be spoilt. Perhaps our chairman on that occasion was exceptional. He knew every one of the thirkty-four people present and we could hear every word he said. The items under discussion were diverse: the smell from the food processing factory, the erection of a village sign, and the siting of four footpath signs. All were matters of considerable interest and discussion. Dissent was vocal but amicable; the most extreme view expressed on the last item was:

"What do we want them for? We'll only encourage interlopers to use our footpaths!"

It also produced some interesting historical notes on footpaths long since disappeared.

Our admirable chairman had remained well in control of the meeting and had brought it to a happy conclusion just in time for most of us the cross the road for a drink.

That whole Parish Meeting had been a neat demonstration of the democratic process in action. On this occasion, here we were back again in the same schoolroom going through the motions of democracy, voting for a member of Parliament.

No election fever, but we did achieve a very high turnout, and most of us got our man in!

Three separate fields along my route contained donkeys. A pair, a family of eight and one solitary moke. In each case they watched my progress with polite interest. The absurd thought came to me that I knew little more about them that they knew of me. the one quite useless fact which I could conjure up was that they are to be found in an encyclopedia between Asquith and Assam. I find it easy to understand the enormous appeal they hold for some people, such as my Aunt Dorothy, for if nothing else they are very photogenic and have a childlike quality. I can quite see that as steam locomotives affect others, they could easily become an obsession. Each holds its own particular charm and even beauty, but neither has much future as a form of transport, which was a subject much on my mind at the time.

I was also surprised that morning to rediscover that a bicycle propelled without undue haste is an even quieter means of progress than walking. I found myself conscious of the silence in the lane and into it came the melody of birdsong. Starlings from the roof of the barn, a thrush high in the sycamore and skylarks even higher over the pasture, untroubled by the presence of a hawk near the old windmill. There were distant sounds of feeding time from the pigs on the other side of the valley and a dog barking over at Blo Norton. There was room for all these sounds along the lane. With the build up of traffic as I neared the village and main road so too the noise level mounted to the muted roar in which we spend so much of our lives.

As I cycled along I suffered a new awareness of the scents on the morning air. Perhaps I was by this time breathing more deeply than usual. I received positive confirmation concerning which of my neighbours along the route keep pigs, and which are the cattlemen. I didn't need confirmation, it was just inescapable.

More surprising than any of these was the offensiveness of motor car exhausts. By the time I panted the last few hundred yards I had become a rabid anti-polutionist, but the warm scent of new baked bread restored the balance of my olfactory nerves, and I knew then that I would soon be back behind a steering wheel, burning up the petrochemicals with the worst of them. The hills of today would become no more than the gear-change of tomorrow.

LOT 12
On the Move

The time eventually arrived when our thoughts began to turn towards retirement. At least mine and those of my wife did; in William's case, he had by then a wife and family to support. We decided to sell up and, in the words of our American friends, relocate.

Now I am sure that everyone has their favourite stories to tell about buying and selling houses. I will record just one telephone conversation which remains vividly in my mind. "We like your house and want to buy it." It was music to my ear. I held the telephone and tried to listen to the effusive chatter which followed. My thoughts went bounding away. After only five weeks with the "For Sale" boards up and 19 viewers behind us, it sounded as if our plans were beginning to come to life with the first essential ingredient about to be offered.

"There's just one thing," I heard, and my spirits sagged. What fly in the ointment could this be? My mind bounced from thatch to drains to cesspit, to the possibility of flooding, or was it just a sordid matter of money?

"Yes," I inquired as gently as I could manage. "Can you tell me," asked the voice to which I was now able to put a face, "what happens in the fields around your property?"

Well, that was a bit of a facer. This was the trick question I thought. Perhaps our whole future depended on getting the answer right. Our prospects seemed suspended by a beanstring. Did she perhaps have an allergy, hay fever, an abhorrence for rural smells, a fear of bulls, or just simple agoraphobia?

"Arable," I said tentatively, "mainly arable, with a little permanent pasture beyond the village where there is a dairy herd." I immediately regretted the dairy herd but hoped that it sounded more acceptable than cows.

"There's some woodland, too, some of it privately managed and some Forestry Commission."

"That sounds find. You see, my daughter is an artist and she wouldn't like to be surrounded by vegetables."

"Well, I think she will be delighted. We had barley in the field over

121

the lane this year, and winter wheat has already been sown for next year.'' I hoped that I was sketching a mental picture of Constable's ''Cottage in a cornfield,'' secluded but not remote, spacious but not too big, unspoiled but well maintained.

I suppose that selling a house is not unlike selling almost anything. One makes them most of what there is to offer, showing it in a favourable light, not wishing to decesive but definitely encouraging the view that one's geese might be swans.

In fact, we still had geese — beautiful, statuesque, useful. At times of normal routine they roamed at will, eating the grass and giving valuable warning when anyone approached. They weren't very helpful in this business of selling the house. I can't say for certain that they actually lost us any potential purchasers though not everybody appreciated that the gander's advances were really defensive. He certainly sorted out the townees from country folk, and that was useful.

If people are used to living in a town, we didn't worry them by telling them about the fox which took the goslings last year, the deer which eat roses, the moorhen whose preferred diet is Cos lettuce and immature brassica. Nor did we alarm them by mentioning the cost of rethatching, the vagaries of cesspits or any such matters which country dwellers accept as normal ingredients of life.

I perfected my guided tour patter but aimed to keep it flexible, stressing the angles which I judged to be most apposite to individual viewers. The package on offer consisted of four buildings of Grade II listed architectural interest. I learned to accept and agree with all suggestions for possible future use.

Yes, the Old Forge would make a very good tea room/restaurant/ studio/drawing office/garage. And yes, the cottage has been well modernised/is delightfully unspoiled/has great scope for improve-ment/needs absolutely nothing done to it. While yes, the small cottage adjacent would be a perfect workshop/granny pad/useful storeroom/ snug little office/or could be demolished to make room for a patio.

Suggestions for the small barn were less enterprising. No one seemed able to conjure up a use more bizarre than its present one. At one end we had the deep freeze and the other end was known as the stripping room. The old bath over which we customarily removed the paint from pine furniture seemed to be a conversation stopper. This was not the case with the thatched roofs. I was told more about thatch from this succession of experts than I ever learned while working with our thatcher or in the years that I maintained it!

Not unnaturally, weekends produced peak viewing times. It was on occasions almost impossible to regulate the confluence of our customers, house buyers, friends, family and weekend guests. I had no particular objection to being viewed while having my morning coffee or while working in the study. Privacy was at a premium but none of us was viewed in bed.

I can vouch that this did happen on our last expedition when we were the hunters instead of the hunted — the teenage son of the house had evidently had a late night. We tiptoed round his guitar and proceeded on course.

Apart from that little cameo I pass quickly by the traumas of house hunting and arrive at the point when William and family had moved into the dereliction of a former pub, our younger daughter and family, whom you have not previously met, were in a large caravan on the forecourt and we, that is my wife and I and the dog, were in another caravan in a field just down the road. We had made it home into Norfolk, but only just!

One other highlight stands out among the memories of those days of toil. A Father and Son plumbing partnership arrived one monring. The younger man was spokesman:

"Dad say to me Arthur, he say, about three years ago I went with your uncle Jack to have a drink at the Gardeners Arms. We got as far as the Swan at Garboldisham and we didn't go no further. Although that were three year ago, I remember them urinals well. Pale blue they was. With all their copperwork polished up they looked real picturesque. They would be just what we want for this job we're doing for Harry! So then we remembered that this ole pub isn't a pub any more and we wondered if them urinals was still here".

They were indeed still there. Their removal was not high on the priority list of jobs to be done although the room itself was destined to become a workshop. The chance to have someone else remove the contrivances and pay for the privilege was fortuitous.

A bargain was struck with both parties well satisfied and that is what I call a good deal.

Working up a ladder on the gable-end of the old pub, I could see the white painted weatherboarding of the post-mill on the south side of the village. A cluster of conifers and a strip of mixed woodland marked the line of the Little Ouse. Beyond was Suffolk and another phase of my life gone downwind.

The next daunting task was rehabilitating the fairly typical old Norfolk pub to create a family home, a place of work and an antique shop. William took over at this point.

We were quite naturally, like incomers to any village, objects of curiosity but it was not long before the more enquiring souls had elicited the main facts. The first one arrived on a bicycle while i was up a ladder. ''Have the old place sold at last?'' He enquired.

''Yiss,'' I answered, slipping back easily into my native tongue.

''What's it going to be then, a hume?''

''A home and an antiques shop.''

''Ah! I thought that wouldnt never be a pub again. It was nice in there though.''

Most of our early visitors were men with clip-boards or a thirst for knowledge. The Postman was the exception.

''Good morning, Mr Hill?'' he greeted me that first morning, but I was not caught by surprise as I had been on a previous occasion. My name was on the envelope in his hand. He soon had us all sorted and pigeon-holed; the young guvnor, the old guvnor and the little old guvnor; three generations gathered together like the half tribe of Manasseh in Gilead.

Some of the knowledge-thirsty visitors, having slaked their own curiosity, went on to give us local information. You might well be of the opinion that giving out unsolicited information is not an East Anglian characteristic. No doubt finding themselves inside the old pub again loosened their tongues even with a complete absence of alcohol.

''This used to be the public, up this end. It wasn't never opened up like this. There was a passage through there to the jug and bottle.''

''Over that side was a sort of snug. Children and little old ladies what didn't like too much noise got in there.''

''They said the wallpaper was white once with sprigs of flowers on it. Nobody didn't believe it till they took a mirror off the wall one day and sure enough you could see it had been white. Fred must have been well over sixty at that time and he said he couldn't never remember the place being tricolated. Of course, that's going back a bit and it's all been done over since then.''

''If you want to know all about this place, you go and talk to Mrs W. along at the thatched cottage. Her father and his before him were landlords here. She can tell you.''

''I've had some happy times in here. Right back to when I started drinking. Wonderful lot of people got in here considering it wasn't a big room before that wall was knocked out. There was a settle along there as well as on this side of the fireplace. That's where the dartboard hung.'' It didn't take a Sherlock Holmes to deduce the last piece of information, the state of the plaster proclaimed many a misthrown dart.

The visitors with clipboard made copious notes and usually talked expansively on such subjects as injection damp-proofing, infestation control, heating, lighting and soundproofing, or, more hopefully, of the availability of grants. Without exception, they all promised to "put something in writing".

As I was often the only person in sight on the job, they each approached me, tentatively enquiring, "Mr Hill?", to which I answered, "Well, yes, but you want the guvnor, he's up in the roof."

I began to enjoy playing my newly acquired subordinate role and passing on the decision making to the young guvnor.

Working up on the ladder gave me a sparrow on the roof top view of the village. At first sight, it doesn't really amount to very much. There is not immediately a lot to see or do, especially if you are in the habit of passing through at great speed on the A1066. Next time I suggest that you slow down and take a more leisurely view; most of the village lies at right angles to the main road.

The commercial centre is easily explored. P.O./Stores, Pub, Garage and Antiques Shop — who could ask for more? Except perhaps a coach load of visitors in need of a cup of tea. In this they will be disappointed unless the driver knows about the garden centre, half a mile down the road to Hopton.

The village sign is surmounted by a model of a post-mill. The real thing is also down the Hopton road, but a most striking distant view of the mill can be enjoyed on the road from Diss as it breasts the last rise before sweeping down into the village. Broomscot Common lies spread out before it, dotted with gorse and blackfaced sheep. From that distance you can't see that they are blackfaced but when you turn left, the road runs beside the common.

The mill has the distinction of being the last remaining one of three in Garboldisham and the only surviving post mill in Norfolk. It was built in the 1770's and apart from time needed to repair storm damage and for work on improved technology such as the fitting of 'patent' sails and cast iron gears, it was in use until 1917. Then followed fifty years of neglect and decay. When the present owner started a programme of restoration in 1972, he had a formiable task ahead of him. Today he is able to operate a milling business in the fully restored roundhouse but there is still much to be done before the full objective of milling by wind-power is re-established.

Nevertheless, it takes only a little imagination when climbing the ladder to the top to recall the sensation of being in a working windmill. It is rather like being between decks aboard a sailing ship. It seems alive with the creak and murmur of timbers taking the strain. There is a gentle but persistent rasp of gear wheels transmitting power from windshaft through brakewheel, wallower, spurwheel and stone-nuts to two pairs of stones. The whole superstructure vibrates and sways gently as the fantail comes into operation to correct for a change in the direction of the wind. The wind sighs eerily and the sails flick through the view of open fields with hypnotic regularity.

It will be a great day when we see sails turning again at Garboldisham but I am not sure that the steep wooden ladders in the dimly lit interior of the mill are just the thing for an elderly people's outing!

Back in the village itself there is, at the crossroads, the war memorial, well sited and tended among lime trees with a back-drop of immense weeping willows. The church of St John the Baptist is as pleasant a parish church as one can find in a very long day's march. It has some good external flint and stone flushwork on the tower which holds six bells and interesting carved pew ends within. You may be lucky enough to see the Ringer's Gotch. It is dated 1703 and its ten quarts capacity indicates that bell ringing is just as thirsty an occupation as visiting villages on a coach outing.

Of All Saints church, only the tower remains, the rest of the building having been demolished in 1734.

On your way round, you will see new homes being built as well as conversion and restoration work; the village is alive and well. Up Back Street, beyond the church, is the village school. There can't be many school buildings more attractive in appearance nor one which disgorges a happier crowd of children.

And that is really the point I wish to make. Garboldisham is a pleasant place in which to work and a happy one in which to live.

We had a hard slog ahead of us but it was work with many moments of fascination, like the morning when with a cascade of crumbling plaster and a crackle of splintering wood, my 'wrecking bar' disappeared into a small black void.

The incident reminded me of a house in North Norfolk which my wife and I viewed when searching for a new home. In the course of our inspection, it became clear that somehow there was a room missing on the ground floor. The answer to our enquiry was, ''Yes, we papered over the door. Mother didn't have no further use for that room''. We lacked courage to pursue the matter and the possibilities haunt us still.

The void into which my jemmy dropped was a mysterious corner of the former Swan public house; an odd part upstairs beside one of the massive chimney pieces. William had said, ''You might investigate that corner. We need to pull those old pipes out and there may be room for the new hot water cylinder.''

Three sacks full of lath and plaster and an unbelieable number of rusty nails later, I had disclosed an ancient doorway which gave into a space about six feet by four. One wall was lath and plaster, one was formed by the sloping side of the brick chimney, the outer wall at that point could be seen as chalk blocks, while the fourth side of the little room was revealed as studwork covered in twentieth century plasterboard.

By the time I had cleared out the place and laid a floor over the joists, I was only just ahead of the heating engineers. A gleaming piece of modern technology now presides in that space which had, I guessed, seen little daylight in the past hundred years or more.

If that particular part of the old pub had remained unchanged for a great many years, the same could certainly not be said of the fireplace in what was destined to be the living room. Haven't we all heard those stories of our friends who have pulled out an old fireplace only to find a still older one behind it? Now it really has happened to me and I have appreciated the excitement of discovery. You need the excitement to compensate for the sheer hard slog, the grime and filth of the soot of ages.

In all, I believe that we removed the remains of six different combustion arrangements; a stove, three fireplaces, a cooking range and a form of water-heater. The inglenook which we eventually reached has splendid curved brickwork at its back. The width is such that we had to remove a much more recently constructed partition wall in order to clear the opening and restore the proportions of the room. Near panic set in when we discovered that the original ten inch square bressemer had been cut through and largely removed. The resulting manipulations involved the use of Accrow jacks, sundry timbers, an R.S.J., a replacement oak beam and, of course, some rather swift bricklaying. My architect son-in-law said that the brickwork only stayed up from force of habit.

The first friend to whom we proudly showed the results of these labours said, "Oh yes! Very lovely, but these big fireplaces are a snare and a delusion; you burn your face while all the rest of the heat goes straight up the chimney."

One of the major difficulties in rehabilitating the Swan was to decide on an order of priorities. On the one hand was the need to hasten work on the domestic side. It is no great fun looking after small children without the sort of amenities which we normally take for granted. The day we achieved a flushing loo was a landmark, followed by a tank of electrically heated water. The next step forward was replacing the gas cylinder and single cooking ring with a splendid cooker which promised to provide hot water to a bathroom of the future and radiators which we were confident would be ready to welcome the chill of autumn.

On the other hand there was the economic pressure to get the showroom area into commission. We opened on schedule but it would be untrue to say that we were really ready to do so. We had debated, long before we moved back to Norfolk, whether we would re-open with a flourish, perhaps a champagne reception? Or whether to do it quietly as our facilities and re-stocking progressed.

As it happened, we were overtaken by events. Even before the sign-writer had finished his work, faithful friends and customers had found us. It was rather like being on stage with the scenery still being erected and painted. "Noises off" were provided by concrete mixer and hammers. The house lights weren't working but we were back in business.

I have mentioned sign-writer and heating engineers; other specialists appeared from time to time but basically this was a monster do-it-yourself operation. Most of the family were involved at some stage or other and an elite band of friends came and helped on high days and holidays. Between them they displayed a fine array of skills, but for sheer artistry and skill none of us could equal Ruben.

Ruben came from down Essex way. Now I don't as a general rule have Essex first in my thoughts about East Anglia, but in the matter of pargetting and ornamental plaster work, Essex has more fine examples than Suffolk, and Norfolk comes a rather poor third.

I had never met an itinerant fibrous plasterer until Ruben suffently drifted in.

There was about the episode a strangely medieval atmosphere. The whole idea of a travelling craftsman arriving unheralded was curiously unlike the twentieth century. So, too, was the informality of the discussion about the work to be undertaken and the striking of a bargain. Board and lodging plus a modest sum of money in exchange for the design and execution of an area of pargetting on the gable end of the building.

Fetching and carrying at his command, we assembled the materials and equipment for the job. First we re-erected our builders tower scaffolding, adjusting and positioning to his satisfaction. This involved having him stand on the platform, swinging his arms and going through the motions of performing his art. He looked like a contender in the early TV parlour game, "What's my Line?" doing his piece of mime to help or confuse the panel.

With this done to his satisfaction, there followed a considerable period of study and contemplation; a viewing of the site from all angles near and far and giving some consideration to the angles of illumination by the rays of the sun on its diurnal course.

At this point it was realised that the sun was at its zenith so a leisurely move was made over the road to the Fox which still offers sustenance and refreshment.

Pargetting on the former Swan public house.

"I don't eat much during the day", said Ruben, but it was soon obvious that even the preparations for plasterwork were exceedingly thirst-making.

Back on the scaffolding, gesturing became even more expansive. He accompanied this activity with little bursts of song and curious incantations. At last the thought process was translated into action. An outline sketch appeared on the wall. His first effort was quickly deemed unsatisfactory, erased and replaced with a second attempt. This was awarded a paeon of self-congratulation and a burst of song.

In a more conventional or traditional pargetting operation, the ornamental work is carried out with the final coating of wet plaster. Modern techniques allow the addition of a water repellent to the mixture of the previous coat. This slows down the drying of the final coating allowing more time for the working of the pattern.

All this, and much more, Ruben told us as he worked, recalling the days before plaster came ready mixed in sacks and chemical additives were unknown. He described with relish how a rich mixture of water

129

and cow dung was slapped on before the final plastering. So far as anyone can establish, this had been the normal procedure since the Saxons were around and started the whole thing.

Ruben's task was to add his relief-work to an established wall surface. He slapped on a liberal coat of bonding material. From my position on the ground, I was glad that it was not cow dung. This he covered with the first of his plaster and that was the end of work for day one. At least it was the end of artistic endeavour. We did persuade him to perform some prosaic 'making good'' inside the old building, but his heart was not in it and his thirst was demanding attention.

Over a pint or two, he willingly recounted memories of his childhood. Mixing plaster ready for 'daubing' took place on site some weeks in advance of requirement. Into a circle of screened sand, a creamy solution of lime was poured. This solution was obtained by adding quick lime to water which bubbled and boiled in a highly dangerous manner. Well beaten cow hair was then added to the creamy mass and mixed well with a long-handled hair hook.

Sand, lime and hair were thoroughly mixed with another long-handled tool called a Larry. "'appy as Larry I was when my dad let me do that''.

Day Two started with a very subdued plasterer working steadily in complete silence. Bit by bit he built up his sculpture. A regal swan gradually took form among a cluster of foliage. The sun began to get hot around midday. Plaster and plasterer were drying fast.

Life after a liquid lunch took on a more relaxed air. Short bursts of song were once again the order of the day; artist took over from sober craftsman. Hawk, float and plasterer's steel were now abandoned. Fine details were sculpted with a small tool carved from hardwood.

Suddenly the magical moment arrived. The picture was complete. Ruben stepped back to admire his work and feel eight feet onto a pile of sand. No bones broken, no plaster required.

LOT 13
Daily Rounds

In the past, I have often used the ''under-sell'' technique, speaking almost slightingly of an item and almost provoking prospective buyers into becoming its champion. Now it seems that I have succumbed to the same method. When they were selling this house to us, they didn't even mention that swifts nested under the tiles. There was no talk of hedgehogs in the garden and they even threw away the old police cell with a passing reference.

I am glad that I have not been everywhere and seen everything and that life is still full of pleasurable little surprises. You may think that I am easily pleased when I say that finding myself having a bath in a former Victorian police cell competed with the delight of realizing that swifts were nesting in the roof of our new home.

New is, of course, a comparative term. The house is new to us but the swifts have undoubtedly been returning here for many generations. They had arrived in April, three months earlier than us. We first heard their screeching and realized only slowly that they were not the more familiar swallows and house-martins. Nesting had long been accomplished and the amount of activity indicated that there were young to be fed. They were using two sides of our roof, zooming in at tremendous speed and disappearing under the pantiles like the last of the bath water going down the drain.

About that bath in the old police cell, when I come to advertise this house for sale, an operation in which we seem to indulge on average every seven years, I shall certainly mention the cell as a unique selling point. The previous owners, I note from their particulars of sale, mentioned it only as ''bathroom with domed ceiling''. This is a real throwaway line which does no justice at all to the most interesting architectural feature of the house. To be a little pedantic, it is not domed but vaulted, with delightful hand-made bricks laid on edge to give a most satisfying surface. The walls are nearly two feet thick, the solid pine door is studded and heavily barred, has a small iron inspection hatch and hinges fit for a castle. A small square window set high in one end of the cell is also barred in the best tradition of all dungeons in every boy's adventure

The Village.

story. The cell and the single room above are recent additions to the house. They were added in about eighteen fifty when it became the village police house. Together they form a solid bastion against which the remainder of the clay lump structure can shoulder for support.

Almost at the same time we moved in, the village once again acquired its own policeman. He lives in a more modern house close to the heart of things. This is our first experience of life in a real village. Previously we have lived in hamlets or splendid isolation and for one quite long period on the edge of a town. No one place can satisfy one's needs or desires at all stages of life. The reason for our moves have been as varied as the houses in which we have lived and always until now have included the need to be within easy reach of the place of work.

Our introduction to life in the village set a standard. On moving day, my wife suddenly said, "I forgot to tell the paper shop that we won't be here after today". Our telephone was still connected so she rang and apologised for not letting the shop know sooner. "That's quite all right, Mrs Hill", they said. "You are moving to Corner Cottage in Cherry Tree Lane, aren't you? We'll be happy to deliver there just the same." This not only set a standard of friendliness but also illustrated and introduced us to the grapevine. We soon discovered that nearly everyone knew all about us almost before we arrived. After quite a short time we find ourselves to be tendrils of the plant, receiving richly informative snippets about all and sundry.

We settled in happily with our new neighbours and house-guests then suddenly, one day in the middle of August, the swifts were gone. The silence after weeks with their calls around us was almost tangible. Suddenly the house-martins had the air space all to themselves and enjoyed a further couple of weeks before they too departed.

It feels like a long time to wait until next April for their return. We will be watching for the in-comers and confidently expect them to return to nest among our rafters. They give us so much pleasure that it seems churlish to mention the one unpleasant aspect of their occupancy. After we moved in, we found some strange insects in our bedroom. They proved to be the parasite which lives on young swifts still in the nest. They apparently do the youngsters little harm and are shed as soon as the fledglings leave the nest. Perhaps that was the moment when the strange creatures sought the warmth of our nest. We made it clear that they were not welcome visitors and they have not bothered us since.

I have not yet entirely retired but I have established a very comfortable half-way style working part-time only. I had not realised just how comfortable nor how well established until suddenly needed again full time.

Usually my mornings are filled happily with an endless procession of fascinating jobs in the workshop, repairing, cleaning and restoring. The items on which I work vary in size from eight feet long doughbins or huge refectory tables to corkscrews, horse-brasses, hand-tools and some which defy name or classification. Its unpredictability is one of the joys of the job. There seem no limits to the flow of antiques, bygones and collectable objects and there is a great satisfaction to be found in their restoration.

You will, I think, readily understand why I am such a happy man. I enjoy my work which is largely with things; inanimate objects which are always interesting and often beautiful. I don't these days have many dealings with people who, lets face it, are not often interesting and are only rarely beautiful. I no longer have to cope with staff and am mercifully free of all involvement with unions. Only occasionally do I meet customers. In fact, I have abdicated successfully from all the cares and worries of running a business. I now potter purposefully and am only mildly saddened that the value added by my activities is taxed at 15%.

So it was quite a shock when holiday time came round and William departed with his family leaving me in sole command.

My briefing was thorough. Four pages of detailed instruction subheaded: Shop, Workshop, Yard and Stockroom, notes on incomplete transactions and forecasts of daily events. It took me quite a while to assimilate that lot. I made my first sale in the shop before reading to the end of the page four — one pair of stickback Windsor chairs. It was not only my first sale that morning but also my last. Other callers included the paper-boy, window-cleaner and the milk lady, all of whom required payments which left me out of pocket by lunch time.

At lunchtime, I went through to the kitchen. I found two more written pages of domestic instructions and requests from my thoughtful daughter-in-law: where to find the gingerbread which she had made for me, which plants needed watering and please remember the hanging baskets and what to expect on Saturday. The mums from the playgroup would arrive to set up a cake stall on the forecourt. And P.S., any cakes left unsold can be offered in the shop until 6.00 p.m. and then placed in the top section of the freezer.

The cake stall project brought the number of cash boxes under my control to four, there already being one each for antiques, local honey and dried flowers.

On the Saturday morning, I got my act together, found the trestle table and chairs for the cake stall, the notice reading 'Home-made Cakes' and a clean tablecloth. I re-read my instructions and realized that I had no milk for the coffee which I would supply at eleven o'clock. Luckily, two pints of goats milk arrived, which I hadn't noticed in the schedule of expected events. There was by then more than enough in the antiques cash box to settle that account. I wondered momentarily if the auditors would accept goats milk as a legitimate business expense.

I was now getting back into the swing of things and overcoming my recently acquired after-lunch drowsiness. I found myself actually looking forward to the next customer and was definitely surprised to find how charming most of them were. Perhaps they always had been and it was only I who had become jaundiced.

It was delightful to hear once again the accents of the Deep South, to recall the friendships which we had made and the transient friends who had moved on to Germany or home to the States. There were a few local characters who wanted to see ''the young man'' and had no need to express in words their obvious feeling that I was unlikely to be of any use. There were those who spoke flatteringly of William and also one or two old friends.

As well as the busy times, there were periods of blissful peace. I sat under an apple tree with a book, largely unread. From there I could hear the crunch of gravel on the forecourt which heralded customers and softened the shock of the bell.

Then, suddenly, the family was home. I was knee deep in grandchildren and slobbered on by the puppy. De-briefing was painless and life returned to normal.

One of the elements of that normality is a walk with the dog after breakfast. Usually my wife and I both go. Sometimes when she has more pressing matters to attend to, Tray and I are despatched on our own. Like yesterday when we met a neighbour he was just setting out for the riding stables where he helps with riding for the disabled.

''Good to be alive on a morning like this'', said Jack, and of course he was right. No matter that the phrase is commonplace. It really was a morning that lifted one's spirits. The almost horizontal rays of a watery sun glistened on every blade of grass, where the moisture of the previous evening had precipitated and turned to crystal.

Honey and Tray are not such good friends as one might wish so extended conversation on these meetings is not possible. Tray and I pressed on over Back Hills.

I am told by my usual impeccable source that I am strange, not being a dog-lover. This may be so but fortunately I am a tolerant person. For more than forty years I have shared the comfort of my home with houseplants, children and dogs. Houseplants can, for the most part, be ignored, children eventually leave home but although dogs' lifespan is relatively short, they are reincarnated in various shapes and sizes. However, I must admit that if it were not for the necessity of a once or twice daily walk, I would miss a great deal of beauty and activity around the village. Take that morning, for example. Blue smoke from a wood fire rose straight into the air on the far side of the fen. Tray and I made our way round over the stream to see what was afoot.

For a moment as we approached the scene of activity, I was disorientated. Then I realised that a whole line of trees which had straddled a ditch was missing. As ever, I was saddened by their loss though they had been trees well past their prime so my sadness will only be rational if their owner fails to plant new ones in their place.

I paused to watch the yellow mechanical monster churning soggy pasture into peat-black mud, swinging tree trunks effortlessly into a pile and pushing more lop and top onto a crackling bonfire. The destruction was awe-inspiring — the skill with which that complicated mechanism was handled was nothing short of artistry.

Where we came up to higher ground, a tractor was at work. Five ploughshares sliced and turned the soil like bow-waves in a muddy estuary. A constantly moving pattern of gulls formed a fluttering wake, starkly white above the fresh-turned soil.

Our way lay between two areas of ploghed land. Both sides had encroached on the grassy track by a full two furrows, leaving a much narrowed path. From the highest point, between bare branches of oak trees, I had a glimpse of the lake, its mirror surface spotted by a gathering of Canada Geese. A heron sketched an erratic flight path along the stream down towards the river.

From that same vantage point on the Suffolk side, I can look back over the fen into a wide sweep of Norfolk. It is a landscape which at first looks to be empty of habitation but there are three churches and a windmill to be picked out among the trees.

A wisp of vapour rose from the dung-heap behind the piggeries as from an ill-snuffed candle. There was a great silence of contentment about the place.

The hedge beside the lane yielded an armful of dead wood. Refusing, as I do, to be entirely deprived of an open fire, my wood burning is no longer a serious matter. It is not much more than a pleasing hobby, the real heat coming from radiators supplied by a central heating boiler.

We met, as we often do, Frank and Henry in the lane. They had a man with them; I don't know his name.

As we came round and back to the village, the single bell on the roof of the chapel-of-ease echoed over the fields. A line of washing hung limp in the still air, its prospects poor. The scent of fresh-baked bread reached us as the daily life of the village got under way. Wheels of industry and commerce were beginning to turn. Sugar beet lorries rumbled through, paper boys were out on their rounds and shopkeepers were opening their doors.

Homeward we went, the old dog and I, past the silent fish and chip shop and the cold granite of the war memorial — unveiled, I have noted, "in the presence of a number of aged and beribboned warriors who in years gone by had served their country on land and sea". (E.D.P. 20th August 1920)

It was all good cliche material which certainly made me feel that it was good to be alive.

"One thing's for sure", I said to my wife the other day, "I can't write much about retirement. I'm too new to it and it isn't funny or specially interesting".

In fact, humdrum is the word that comes to my mind. It's a word my Producer at Pebble Mill used recently when rejecting my latest story for radio. "Utterly humdrum," he said. (It sounds much better in a Northumberland accent). "I can't imagine anyone listening to it for fifteen minutes."

You, who know me better than does my Producer, would recognise it instantly as an autobiographical story. You would certainly recognise the village in which it was set, the route into the City and the supermarket in which some of the action took place.

Philip, my surrogate hero, was sitting at the breakfast table reading his morning paper.

"I hope you are not going to sit around getting in my way all the time. Just because you have retired, it doesn't mean that I have any less to do." He lowered his paper and sketched a reply but before he could fill in the details, Sylvia had picked up the tray and disappeared into the kitchen. He put down the paper and followed her to the sink.

"Of course," he said, "I only retired yesterday and it may take a little time to work out a new routine. I did think that I might be able to help you a bit so that we could have more free time together."

The thought of Philip doing anything useful around the house was one which needed digesting. Sylvia realised that it was more than half her fault. She had always run a smoothly efficient household in which there had been little place or call for male participation. Even now the

137

daily help carried much of the load while Sylvia organised and perfected with the ease of long practice. She thought about his offer as she put cups and saucers in the rack. Philip inspected the washing machine as if seeing it for the first time.

"Well," she said at last, "You could try your hand at doing some shopping. I usually go to the supermarket on Thursday mornings. If you take my list and do that, I can clear several jobs here this morning and then we could have lunch together at about one."

Philip departed with the shopping list and several verbal footnotes. Driving past the riding stables, the expression "out to grass" came to his mind. He didn't like it and glanced quickly in the driving mirror to see if he really looked long in the tooth. The well trimmed ex-Army man looked back at him reassuringly.

He rather liked the supermarket. It appealed to his orderly mind; the whole atmosphere was quite different from the little corner shop where he customarily shopped or the hardware shop in the high street. At short notice, he couldn't actually recall visiting any other shops though he supposed he must have done so.

Providing himself with a trolley and clutching his list, he set forth into the unknown. He was deighted to note that he had collected every item on the list in eight and a half minutes, less pleased that it was necessary to record almost the same period of waiting time at the check-out queue, where he followed the example of the woman ahead of him, selecting a stout looking cardboard carton.

"Put your flaps up, dear", said the check-out operator, "it will hold more that way." Well, Philip was fairly quick on the uptake so he got the flaps of the 12 x 25 fluid oz special value carton pulled up and was able to get all his purchases into it.

As he left the checkout, he ought to have put his hands under the carton. He didn't and the bottom fell out. The contents, including half a dozen bottles of Guinness, six eggs and two large size cartons of natural yoghurt crashed on the simulated marble floor.

It was like swearing in church. There was a sudden awesome hush. Philip felt all eyes in his direction. Luckily he was old enough not to be embarrassed easily but was momentarily at a loss. What happened was that he immediately became the recipient of the greatest possible help and kindness. In no time at all, the Manageress, three assistants and one cleaner converged on him and started a restoration job.

He and his dripping debris were whisked into a side room. A clean cloth was offered to wipe the egg from his shoes and trousers. His undamaged groceries were repacked in a fresh cardboard box and all the spoiled items were replaced free of charge.

138

"Are you all right?"

"Would you like to sit down?"

"Do have a cup of tea."

He began to think that he had been knocked down by a car and was suffering a temporary loss of memory. But the point which really struck home was that those fine, competent women were blissfully happy putting to rights a hapless male who was so clearly out of his element. They were secure in a state of ascendancy. It started Philip on a downward path of awful doubts about male superiority.

That was the basis of the story you will not be hearing. I had held a mirror up to life. It reflected no great drama, no fantasy, no conflict, just some real people and places; entirely normal, satisfyingly humdrum.

The very first morning in our present home I answered the postman's knock on the front door.

"Good morning, Mr Hill?" he enquired. It was not his fault that one of the letters delivered on that first day was a rate demand. He was of course checking on a new arrival in his ambit and indirectly drawing attention to the inadequate letterbox in our front door.

The door itself probably antedates Rowland Hill's penny post and the miserable slot cut in it at a much later date was well below any current British standards. It was certainly too small to accommodate International "A" sizes, company reports, Sundays papers or those of my manuscripts which come home to roost. Replacement didn't get a high priority among the many works of alteration and restoration in which we were engaged. After all, it is quite compatible with the quaint Victorian collection box set in our garden wall, and into which we are unable to post anything larger than old-fashioned quarto.

From my own limited experiences of door to door deliveries, I place the letterbox fairly high on the postman's list of daily hazards. I have been surprised by the number which don't exist at all and the very high proportion of inadequate ones. The jammers and finger-snappers are not uncommon and the modern horror at grovelling ground-level in the glass front door is not only bad for lumbago but also an undignified arrangement.

One of my happiest moments during the drudge of leaflet delivery occurred when I met two ladies who were working the street in the opposite direction. "What are you on this week, Love? We're doing Daz!" I was doing a party political and I wondered whether or not it got a better reading than the commercial; there were similarities.

But leaflet delivery is easy in as much as the actual address matters not at all; it's one for each house regardless. Even individually addressed deliveries are relatively simple in the towns where streets are named and houses numbered, but try and find such as "Barn Cottage, Buxtead". Of course if you can find someone to ask it will be easier — there is always someone watching you even if you can't see them — but if you can find someone, mention the name of the owner rather than the name of the house, and you'll be told in an instant.

"Oh! You're looking for Edward's, why you can see it from here, or could but for the barn."

I'm never too sure about this business of giving a name to a house, except where one flows naturally from its appearance or position. Quite clearly a name becomes a shorthand word picture, its interpretation depending on one's own associations and experiences. I feel that I can have a good guess at the origin of many. I suspect that the Lynmouth's, Ringwood's and their ilk are usually honeymoon locations and I am more than suspicious that the Hersanmine's and Bertanmay's are quietly cocking a snook at the Rhydall-waters and the Derwent. In this parish I give the prize for originality to Costa la Fortune — a cri de coeur if ever I heard one.

No doubt our cheerful postman accepts our eccentricities as efforts to display our individuality, but they must present a newcomer to the round with some difficulty when he sorts our letters before starting out from what we used to call the General Post Office. (The General was, I tell myself, retired or eliminated to meet the requirements of fashionable egalitarianism, and thinking back to those days of Empire the title certainly had Imperial overtones out of keeping with the house colours).

When I was checking our entries on the electoral roll recently, I was intrigued to note some of the variations in address within the village where we live. Three neighbouring houses in one road were listed, each of us giving the road a different name, and one householder in the lane beside us gave the lane a name which I have not met elsewhere.

"A Good Address" is not a phrase much used today. It has no exact counterpart even in the language of estate agents — "a much sought after or desirable neighbourhood" fails to carry quite the same standing or delicious snobbery of "a good address". Perhaps this is what we are seeking when we put together a euphonious address without too fine a regard for correctness.

Now advancing technology has reached us and we have received our orders. Luckily I am well versed in these matters. When the next uniformed representative of the service knocks at the door and enquires "Mr Hill?", I shall spring to attention and answer smartly "IP22 1DL. Sir!"

Not all the changes we find around us are easily assimilated. The first time I went unwittingly into a Unisex hairdressers I suffered a severe emotional shock. My overwhelming impression of that particular establishment was that they were more concerned with sex than haircutting. Asking for a short back and sides was like ordering one of cod and a small portion of chips with vinegar in the Carlton Grill. I was lucky to get away with only a coloriser rinse and blowdry to complete my junior executive-style cut. I took a shower at the earliest opportunity to rid myself of a pervasive adour of Aujourdui du Printemps, or was it Dejune sur l'herbe?

You will appreciate that I am somewhat set in my ways when it comes to matters such as a haircut. I used to get exactly what I wanted at Mr Cousen's shop in Red Lion Street, just off the Gentleman's Walk in Norwich. The service cost sixpence and that included use of the mechanical rotary brush driven from a pulley on an overhead shaft. Conversation on the subject of the weather, horses or the prospects of the Canaries for next Saturday was optional. I usually opted out and was well served all the years that I was able to continue visiting the estabishment.

Following those early days, I had no serious tonsorial trouble either at boarding school or later in the army though I can't say that I ever actually enjoyed or could commend their institutional arrangements.

Since those far off days, my fading hair has been cut and has fallen on a variety of floors, mostly linoleum covered. One landmark stands out in my mind. At Sudbury, a young man just started in the business, incorrectly assumed me to be a pensioner and charged me a special cheap rate. I appreciated the cut-price but was saddened to realize that I was thinning on the top and already looked like an O.A.P.

Now, fourteen years and two moves later, all our daily needs are supplied in the village which holds a choice of grocer and greengrocer, a multiple choice of public house, a butcher, fish and chip shop and a choice of hairdresser. I go to Shirley's, a scant two minutes' walk from my own front door. I make an appointment and receive the quickest and most charming attention of all the long line of tonsorial artists on whom I can look back.

The speed and dexterity of Shirley's scissor work is breath-taking. We exchange a few pleasantries and comments on the life of the village. I am not troubled by having to make decisions prompted, as they used to be, by such questions as "Would you like a little something on it, sir?" and it is certainly not suggested that I might care to purchase any of that range of goods which was traditionally offered for sale by my old short-back-and-sides practitioners.

Of course, we don't speak of short back and sides. What I have is a dry-styling and my old friend Mr Cousens would be amazed at what sixty years has done to the price.

My wife tells me that, generally speaking, women don't like to be seen with their hair in a state of disarray or under the drier so I am always careful not to recognise any of the other customers. In this I am helped by my glasses steaming up as I enter the warm, moistly scented atmosphere of Shirley's Salon. For the same reason, I would find it difficult to read any of the magazine provided if I was ever kept waiting. I can tell from their glossy covers that among them I would not find the familiars of yesteryear such as Tit-bits and Everybodys.

Nor is Shirley's the only new face to brighten the more routine occasions of life. Just the other day my wife said:

"You don't usually polish your shoes when you are going to the dentist."

"No," I replied, "but then you haven't seen my new dentist."

I am filled with sadness when I think of all the occasions I have spent over the years dreading visits to my dentists. I realise, too, that there has been a psychological change which now dispels the dread and actually causes me to remember my appointments rather than close my mind and forget the whole business.

There was one dentist, long ago, of whom I can think without a shudder. I even remember him with a small twinge of nostalgic pleasure for if one was lucky enough to get the last appointment of the day, a glass of sherry followed his official ministrations. But he was much my senior and I sometimes thought his eyesight was failing.

All the others I think of as hairy apes, not deeply endowed with feelings of common humanity or natural tenderness. My first encounter with the needle in the hands of the Royal Army Medical Corps left me out cold on the concrete floor at the very beginning of my army career. It has taken me nearly fifty years to overcome that trauma. Even the well-meaning character who used to creep up on me from behind the chair with syringe half concealed behind his back before making an ugly lunge; even he brought me out in a cold sweat. He was a genius compared with the ham-fisted operator who failed three successive attempts to locate the right nerve and finally brought his partner in to anaesthetize me. I can still see that colleague in my mind's eye, he looked exactly like Captain Birds Eye and I can almost swear that he danced a hornpipe just before I drifted into numbness. It was perhaps marginally better when I was given a general anaesthetic although I always had an uncomfortable fear of what I might say while under the influence of the gas. The possibilities of this came home to me when I first noticed ill-concealed smirks around me as I regained my faculties. On another occasion I was told that I had just re-enacted the siege of Malta.

So you can see that one way and another, I was more than a little enchanted when I walked in all unprepared to find a new, charming, tender, caring, female dentist. Her hands are firm and gentle, she smells ever so slightly of French perfume instead of disinfectant, pipe tobacco and golf clubs. She has a nice sense of humour, not boisterous, hearty, doctor-in-the-house knock-about, something altogether more subtle and soothing.

She easily talked me into have some of my missing teeth replaced. Now, it's strange that I detect a stubborn reticence on the subject of dentures. This seems odd in such a blatantly permissive age when all parts of the body and their functioning are subjects of open discussion and comment, and variously displayed in papers and magazines and thrust at us on our television screens. Yet even the 'commercials' fight shy of showing actual sets of dentures. I find this remaining taboo left over from Vioctoriana the more inexplicable considering that no-one blinks at the idea of needing spectacles to aid sight, hearing aids for the hard of hearing, nor artificial limbs, hearts, kidneys, cosmetic surgery and not even artificial insemination.

Clearly false teeth need a supporters' club and all the paraphernalia of P.R. and propaganda to make them acceptable. It shouldn't need much of a pressure group to abolish this hang-up to loosen our tongues and allow us to click and smile unselfconsciously.

In all I paid a series of five visits. When I returned home after the final fitting, with six new teeth, a haircut and with my shoes polished. I was quite surprised that old dog recognised me.

There had to be a serpent in this dental garden of Eden. It arose in the form of a growing discomfort which took me back for a sixth visit to the surgery.

"Hello," she greeted me, "are they in your mouth or in your pocket?"

They were in my pocket. I restored her crestfallen response to this by telling her about my wife. She, I explained, was actually pleased that I had at last had cause for complaint. Up till then I had stoked fires of jealousy with my paeons of praise for my new dentist.

Perhaps I should have kept my mouth shut, or as on another memorable occasion, have thought carefully before I spoke. The conversation was running like this:

"Do you understand why you are here?"

"Steady, David," I warned myself, "give the wrong answer and you will find yourself in a psychiatric ward."

The question came at the end of a long catechism in the course of which the state of most of my bodily functions had been questioned.

Given time I could have replied that "Yes, I'm here so that you can find out what is wrong with me and hopefully provide a cure." In fact, I was in no state for quick repartee or well phrased replies so I only mumbled something about my G.P. playing for safety.

I cannot be entirely trusted to recall the events of that day with any great accuracy. My wife, as usual, is a more reliable source.

Things diverged from the normal when I passed out, sitting up in bed about to start my breakfast. In the course of that exhibition, half a pint of coffee went over the bed and later in the day my wife found her bedroom slippers well lined with marmalade.

Now, it is very sad these days to hear so much adverse criticism of the N.H.S. My experience shows this to be an illfounded exercise. I note for the record that our doctor was at my bedside in a matter of minutes and that in not many more minutes I was installed in a hospital bed.

There, of course, the fun starts as one is assimilated into the system, with comprehensive documentation a prerequisite to medication. It all seems very tedious at the time when one's sole desire is to get one's head down on a pillow and in some way be put out of one's misery. When feeling less ill, the daily round is killingly funny. (Whoops! I mean exceedingly funny. I'm having trouble with my adjectives though I don't suppose that was recorded on the clip-boarded chart which hung at the foot of my bed.)

Slotted into each twenty-four hours, there are brief episodes of peace and quiet. not too many, just enought to punctuate the full and recurring daily routine. And there are doctors, too — one almost forgets about them in what you might call the domestic life of the ward.

Visiting time comes round at least once a day. It is a bitter-sweet occasion. We would be bitterly sad and sorry if they didn't come but the peace and quiet when the visitors have all left is very sweet. Conversation is generally over-hearty and hard to sustain. One solution is to have sufficient visitors for them to be able to talk happily among themselves. There is all-round relief when the bell sounds for visitors to depart. We settle into our pillows, close our eyes and enjoy the moment.

But, of course, it doesn't last long. My wife advises that the way to survive in hospital is to take a cat-nap whenever the opportunity occurs. Good advice, though I suspect that she forgets that my hospital admissions exceed hers by an uncomfortable margin. Perhaps she discounts army hospitals as all part of the service.

I couldn't possibly forget 90th General Hospital, set high up in the centre of Malta. Ward M4 was the most comfortable billet I found in

144

my army career even though I did suffer yellow jaundice, sandfly fever, dysentery, dermatitis and scarlet fever. The latter was a strange affliction as I was the only recorded case on the island. I was isolated and scrutinized by a great many members of the R.A.M.C.

Having experienced isolation, I do not hesitate to state my preference for a bed in a ward. Even noises at night do not sway my choice. It is easy to see that a hospital is an irresistible setting for television drama. The whole world struts on its stage where true life is often more dramatic than fiction. I have seen life and death in the wards. I have learned humility and a great deal besides.

There are certain advantages to be found in civilian hospitals as compared with military. In the West Suffolk, for example, we don't have a Commanding Officer's inspection at eleven hundred hours every morning. I clearly remember being ordered not to disturb the alignment of carefully turned down sheets and I still recall that the kicking of bed castors into perfect echelon had a unique juddering effect on fevered patients. My favourite memory of those daily inspections was one morning, after a night of air-raids, the C.O. marched in.

Good morning, Matron. Any windows broken? Anybody killed?''

Life is a deal more civilised in West Suffolk General. As a result of all these recent experiences I am, I fear, like Philip, on a downward path of awful doubts about male superiority.

LOT 14
Low Tech. High Tech.

I am not sure if it is a matter of pride or of sorrow to be able to recall travelling on the old Southwold railway, but it is certainly a source of immense pleasure returning to places of such happy childhood memories.

A roadbridge over nothing much but a bed of nettles didn't seem like a very promising start. It did, however, prove that we were on the course of the old railway line and it seemed a good enough place at which to begin our journey back.

To be truthful, it is not difficult to find, as most of it is marked on the O.S. map. The railway was built in 1879, it has been disused for over fifty years, and in many places is no easier to find on the ground than a Roman road perhaps two thousand years old.

The start of the narrow gauge is easily found in Halesworth alongside the Great Eastern line where goods and passengers transferred for the journey down to the coast. Beyond the two railway bridges, in Quay Street, we will soon look in vain for the origins of such a name. The vast waterside warehouses are disappearing and the Wherry seems almost as far from a natural habitat as does the Oriental on the other side of the street.

Only a trickle of the river Blyth remains to remind us of the former navigation up from the sea, along nine twisting miles and through four sets of locks.

The demise of both these commercial routes has allowed the valley to revert to a scene of pastoral peace.

The old railway track provides rough walking until Blythburgh is in sight, but from here on it leads right into the heart of breathtaking beauty of a kind hardly known outside Suffolk. We followed into Tinkers Walks, with sweeping views across the widening estuary. Over Walberswick Common the tall white lighthouse at Southwold acted as a leading mark away over the marsh and common.

There was no need for us to pick up the key which would have ensured our safe passage of the single track over the former swing-bridge, for now a footbridge only spans the tidal waters. We walked on through the only cutting of this little line and arrived at the site of the station where passengers used to climb down from the tramlike carriages to the low platform.

There was no horse-bus waiting for us, so we walked up the street, footsteps in the present, memories in the past.

My wife has her own recollections of Southwold of times when, as a child, she spent summer days with her grandparents at their holiday cottage, Jersey Lodge, overlooking the Green.

Jersey Lodge, still with its flagpole fixed in a businesslike manner by my wife's step-grandfather, looks out towards Gun Hill.

From all accounts that I have heard, Alfred Buckland was a step-grandfather of great gentleness and kindness to a small girl with an enquiring mind. He was also something of an engineer and inventor, who narrowly missed making a fortune with his own version of a hot water geyser. I have inherited and use some of his metal and woodworking tools. It gave me a jolt recently to see identical tools in a centenary exhibition of bygones at North Walsham.

Our wanderings took us down Ferry Road with best forgotten memories of the '53 flood, to the harbour mouth and the old ferry crossing place.

We sat eating our picnic lunch watching the exertions of the ferryman pulling people to and from the Walberswick side. I would find it easy to believe if told that the old steam driven ferry had slipped its chains and gone to Dunkirk but I believe that our old friend became a less heroic victim of the war.

Back in the town, we sought out the delightful little museum and indulged in an orgy of reminiscences — ''anecdotage'' our children call it. My wife tried to establish the whereabouts of the Zoo, remembered from very early days; this presented some difficulties but I must not tell her story.

In the little museum I came upon a photograph of a rather unusual windmill. It was said to have been in existence in 1938 but I could find no trace of it. My enquiries produced the information that this pump had stood over a reservoir at the head of a tidal creek on the south side of the town. It appears that the plunger pump worked by the windmill lifted the saltwater into a trough which delivered its flow to the evaporating pans of a salt works.

Thinking of my years in Malta and visits to other places around the Mediterranean area, it always struck me at the time that using the hot sunshine to evaporate sea water in extensive pans was eminently sensible and economical. Those pans had usually been hewn from the solid rock and the gathering of the dried out crystals presented few problems. I suspect that today pollution could well be a difficulty not easily overcome.

I found it hard to believe that such conditions could ever have existed at Southwold, or for that matter anywhere else along our East Coast. However, the Domesday Survey of Suffolk of 1087 recorded twenty salt pans in Suffolk, seven of these being around Great Yarmouth. In fact, of course, conditions didn't exist in quite the same way. The warmth rather than the heat of the sun was used in conjunction with the drying winds to concentrate the salt water, the brine solution was then reduced to crystals by artificial heat.

The saltworks at Southwold seem to have suffered various vicissitudes but to have been more or less active right into this century when the Southwold and London Trading Company bought it and became the last operators. They were not able to compete with larger firms in the bulk production of coarse salt for the fishing or chemical industries. They were for a short time able to use their expertise refining rock salt brought from Cheshire. No doubt some of it was carried on the now long defunct Southwold railway.

So far as I have discovered, there are not more than half a dozen manufacturers of salt in the U.K. today. The nearest of these is just down the coast at Maldon. Like the others formerly found along the coast, it has its origins in Roman times. Unlike any of the others today, the Maldon works is the only one still producing sea salt for table use.

The method remains the same in principle as it always has. The differences lie in the materials from which equipment is made. Stainless steel vats have replaced earthenware crocks as evaporation vessels. Wood and coal for firing have given way to North Sea gas which is a rather poetic touch.

In spite of advanced techniques of measurement and control, the traditional arts of boiling are still important. Among others, these include an ability to listen and act upon the tell-tale sounds of the hot pan in the latter stages of evaporation and keeping a knowledgeable watch on the surface as the salt crystals begin to form.

Earlier, during the galloping boil, impurities will have risen to the surface as a froth known as the lees. This will have been skimmed off with a perforated copper skimmer.

When boiling has been completed, the pans are allowed to cool and are then 'drawn'. This entails carefully raking the crystals to the side of the pan with wooden 'hoes' and is followed by progressive drying. Wooden shovels, similar to those used by maltsters, are used when transferring the crystals to each subsequent stage.

It is easy to see how such a laborious process was unable to compete with the comparatively straightforward mining operations in Cheshire.

There were no huge subsidies from the tax-payers, no fraternal aid from Siberia; pans fell into disuse and the industry died a natural death. Only the efficient specialists survived. As with any ancient craft we were always keen to track down the traditional tools of the trade. In this case we were far too late on the scene.

Now that we are no longer in the business folk museums and exhibitions of bygones still continue to enthral us. Perhaps more so as we have time to seek them out and enjoy them.

There was a specially good exhibition at the East of England Show one year. Instead of being a carefree visitor, I was an Exhibitor. At least, that is stretching things a bit — I was really standing-in at short notice for a friend. Almost overnight I became a salesman of Executive Desks and Hi-tech style office furniture. This was quite a change from antiques and bygones. It also transgressed what I believe to be a couple of basic tenets for salesmen; that of having a thorough knowledge of your product or service, and a comprehensive understanding of the back-up organisation behind you. These are not newfound truths, but part of what I was taught in the thirties while on a Pitman's Intensive Business course. However, I did my homework and tried to get it right.

This isn't just sales-talk, my friend's firm really is a very interesting set-up, producing most beautiful wood products alongside more mundane items. Being housed in a converted barn on the Norfolk/Suffolk border, and providing employment for six craftsmen, the firm comes within the ambit of C.O.S.I.R.A., so there we were on the showground among a tented galaxy of rural crafts and small industries.

Our interesting and friendly neighbours included Potter, Sculptor, Taxidermist, Furniture Restorer and, most picturesque of all, a Coppice-worker and Bodger. We were downwind from the Farriers, which was noticeable at times of hot shoeing. The ring of hammer on anvil was sometimes lost among the clamour of a West Indian steel band. Pleasant scents carried to us on the breeze varied from hot doughnuts and fish and chips on crushed wet grass and warm horses.

On the first morning it took the two of us some time to put the final touches to our display. We sorted out our sales literature, hung wall display photographs, polished the furniture and finally arranged the large bunch of mixed flowers picked from the garden at 6 a.m. that morning. It would be fair to say that both my colleague and I are of the military style of flower arranger, with a "get in there, stand up straight and get your hair cut" attitude to floral arrangement. We thought they looked good and added a human dimension to the rather stark atmosphere of efficiency.

With all this behind us, it was time to turn our attention to the potential customers who were beginning to drift by. Straight in at the deep end, with no time for flutters of stage-fright, I was launched into my new line of sales talk. "… a versatile trolley-desk … extending shelf to accommodate computer keyboard … room for disc drive and print unit … locking panel for complete security." I really did know about the trolley-desk and the supporting range of office furniture presented no difficulties. The trouble was that damned computer!

In the light of experience I am able to confirm that the average computer expert is four feet tall and twelve years old. In their droves they spotted our machine and homed in on it, flooring me with their questions, running their grubby fingers over the keyboard and seemingly only slightly put out by the information that the hardware would cost them three thousand pounds. Sadly I confessed to successive buffs that I knew little of computers but with brightening eyes and rising confidence I claimed to know everything about trolley-desks and Hi-tech office furniture.

When I was able to take a break I walked across the showground to the sheep-pens to rusticate for a few minutes and to talk to a friend. As always, I enjoyed watching the crowds almost as much as the exhibits. It was clear why the East of England is a three day show, it would take all that time to see everything even without events in the rings. It is a show which has something for everyone and I could believe that nearly everyone was there. Something was different about these people which I couldn't entirely define. Thinking about it now, perhaps it was more of an urban crowd, and, come to think of it, they didn't talk like yew an' me.

So then it was back to the Hi-technology, the demonstrations and the smooth talk, Was I any good at it?

Well, I was invited to give a repeat performance and we finished a series of exhibitions that year in London at the Agricultural Hall, Islington.

It sounds like a contradiction of terms, Islington today being about as far removed from agriculture as anything that I can think of.

Since being refurbished, this remarkable building has been renamed The Business Design Centre. Those of us who remember the old days are apt to refer to it as the Old Aggie, a name perpetuated by the Aggie Bar in one corner of the gallery. Up in the opposite corner is the Designers' Club. In each of these you will find the city suits, briefcases and furled unbrellas have long since taken over from boots, Norfolk jackets and bucolic farmers.

My memories of the place date from 1937 when I attended a Laundry

150

Southwold.

Engineers and Allied Trades Exhibition at the start of my career in that industry. On this latest occasion the places of Davey Paxman boilers, Baker Perkins machinery, Ruston and Hornsby steam engines and the like were taken by the exhibits of Design for Offices 88. The scene was very different, strictly up to the minute Desking Systems, Graphic Design, vending machines, Data systems, Computer design equipment and every conceivable office ancillary service and supply from contract lighting to waste bins.

My small part in this galaxy was played out in a supporting role on Stand 13 on the Mezzanine floor — three days of persuasive talk, soft sell, of making friends and influencing people, hard on the voice, even harder on the feet. The next few months, as the orders rolled in, proved the extent of our success.

There was however no shadow of doubt about the success of my second venture in Town. I have a diary which in addition to the usual map of the Underground has maps of Theatreland and Clubland. With the help of these I found my way to the Garrick Club and the fulfilment of a longstanding invitation to dine.

This was, I may say, my first visit to such an august establishment. It is a retreat, a haven of solid comfort and good fellowship. If you detect a faint air of levity in my remarks, it is because this club is almost a caricature of itself. It gives life and breath to all those old jokes in Punch; all the characters are there in their ageing eccentricity; everything seems slightly larger than life. The ornateness of the building, the grand staircase, the proliferation of portraits of illustrious members past and present and a veneration of the even more famous founder (1717-79), depicted in two and three dimensions in a curious variety of roles.

What more can I say? Bar and menu were both of notable length, the service impeccable, my host a model of old world courtesy. I remember that evening as a charmed occasion; a counterpoise to my other world of computers, office efficiency and my Filofax friends at the Old Aggie.

I nearly forgot to mention that just over the road from the Old Aggie lies Camden Passage. The passage is the hub, the heart of the antiques world. If you get up early you will find my sister-in-law there. Mention my name and you might get trade discount.